Eyewitness
VOTE

Ballot box, Spanish
Royal Academy

French
revolutionary
dress, 1790s

United Nations
peace sculpture

Badge of state
security police,
East Germany

PASSPORT

Nelson Mandela, elected South
Africa's first black president

Passports, a proof
of citizenship

Portrait of Oliver Cromwell,
Lord Protector of the English
Commonwealth, 1653–1658

Eyewitness
VOTE

Written by
PHILIP STEELE

A rosette in party colors, worn
by party members during
election campaigns

The Capitol, Washington, DC,
home of the US government

DK Publishing

Academy Award, voted for by the
motion picture industry

Bust of George Washington,
first president of the United
States, 1789–1797

Soviet badge showing the
hammer and sickle

Ceremonial mace used in the UK's
House of Commons

DK

LONDON, NEW YORK,
MELBOURNE, MUNICH, AND DELHI

Consultant Professor David Miller

Project editor Clare Hibbert
Art editor Neville Graham
Managing art editor Owen Peyton Jones
Managing editor Camilla Hallinan
Art director Martin Wilson
Publishing manager Sunita Gahir
Category publisher Andrea Pinnington
Picture research Sarah and Roland Smithies
DK picture library Rose Horridge, Romaine Werblow
Senior production editor Vivianne Ridgeway
Senior production controller Man Fai Lau
Jacket designer Andy Smith

DK DELHI
Art Director Shefali Upadhyay
Designer Govind Mittal
DTP Designer Harish Aggarwal

First published in the United States in 2008 by
by DK Publishing , 375 Hudson Street, New York, New York 10014

08 09 10 11 12 10 9 8 7 6 5 4 3 2 1
ED600 – 01/08

A catalog record for this book is
available from the Library of Congress.

ISBN: 978-0-7566-3382-0 (Hardcover)
978-0-7566-3381-3 (Library Binding)

Color reproduction by Colourscan, Singapore
Printed and bound in Hong Kong by Toppan Printing Company Ltd

Discover more at
www.dk.com

Contents

Bronze voting tokens from ancient Athens, after 500 BCE

The people's choice

WHO WILL WIN the Indian general election? People argue on street corners. Newspapers are filled with headlines about one party or another. Politicians are interviewed on television. However, in the end, only the voters can choose how they are governed. More than a billion people live in India, and all over this vast country they line up at polling stations—business people in the busy streets of Mumbai, farmers in hot, dusty villages, and fishermen by tropical harbors. A political system in which the government is chosen by the people in free elections is called a democracy—and India is the world's largest.

DEMOCRACY AND LIBERTY
A statue commemorates Mohandas K. Gandhi (1869–1948). Gandhi organized a nonviolent campaign against British rule in India, which had begun in 1858 and lasted until 1947. Once India could govern itself freely, democracy could take root.

OUR TURN TO VOTE
Women from the northwestern state of Rajasthan line up to vote in India's 2004 general election. The election was held in five regional stages over three weeks. Nearly 380 million Indians voted in this election, out of 675 million registered voters. They could vote at one of 700,000 polling stations.

VOICES OF DISSENT
Workers in childcare centers take to the streets of New Delhi in 2007 in protest against Indian government policy. Voting enables people to choose representatives or policies and to have a say in the decisions that affect their lives. However, new policies that satisfy the majority may upset a minority of people. A wise government listens to the voices of dissent as well as those of its supporters.

DEMOCRACY AND JUSTICE
Democracy may be fairer than other ways of organizing government, but it does not guarantee a just society. For thousands of years, India has been divided into strict social classes called castes. In 2006, when the Indian government suggested reserving some college places for poor people from the lowest castes, these medical students from Amritsar protested strongly: they believe that university admission should be based on ability alone.

PARTY VICTORY

Waving flags and posters, supporters of the Indian National Congress Party celebrate the victory of their leader Sonia Gandhi in 2006. She had resigned from parliament after accusations of misconduct, and then ran in a by-election, held between general elections to fill a vacant seat in parliament. Political systems with different parties are called multiparty or pluralist systems.

HOUSE OF THE PEOPLE

Up to 552 elected representatives sit in the Lok Sabha ("House of the People"). It is one of the two assemblies that make up the Indian Parliament. The other is the Rajya Sabha ("Council of States").

Candidate's details

Party logo

Electronic voting machine (EVM)

Keypad

LOK SABHA

Ballot Unit

A VOTING MACHINE

Electronic voting machines (EVMs) were used in India's 2004 general election. The candidates are listed next to their party logo. Voters press a pad next to their choice. In 2004, the Indian National Congress won 216 seats, the Bharatiya Janata Party (BJP) won 186 seats, and other political parties won 137 seats.

Why people vote

LEAVING IT TO CHANCE
Drawing straws is one way to make group decisions. Everyone has an equal chance of picking the short straw. Some ancient Greek officials were chosen by lottery. Chance is fair, but it does not allow people to make an informed choice.

VOTING IS A WAY of making decisions. Even in a small group of people, such as a family, decision-making can be hard. It is even harder to reach agreement within larger groups, let alone in society as a whole. Such questions as "What should be done?", "How should it be done?", or "Who should do what?" can lead to indecision or arguments. One way to resolve conflict and move forward is to make proposals on which everyone can vote. The basic principle of democracy is that every vote counts equally, and the proposal that gets the most votes in its favor is adopted.

Raised hand signals "yes"

ARE WE ALL AGREED?
Workers at a French factory raise their hands to show that they agree to a strike proposal. A direct, public vote on policy by a show of hands is only possible if the meeting or assembly is small enough for the votes to be counted accurately.

ORANGE REVOLUTION
A multiparty democracy can accommodate violently opposed political parties. Ukraine's 2004 presidential election was bitterly disputed. Supporters of Viktor Yuschenko (above) protested that the election of Viktor Yanukovych (whose supporters are shown right) was rigged. The election was rerun, and this time Yuschenko was declared the winner.

Reverend Ian Paisley (DUP), first minister of Northern Ireland

SHARING POWER FOR PEACE
If a state is torn apart by conflict, government may have to be shared between the opposing sides. In 2007, old enemies from Sinn Féin and the Democratic Unionist Party (DUP) agreed to work side by side in the Northern Ireland Assembly.

Martin McGuinness (Sinn Féin), deputy first minister of Northern Ireland

NO VOTES, NO FREEDOM

Some governments rule without fair elections or even representation of the people. Governments that hold complete or absolute power are called totalitarian. In 1949 British writer George Orwell imagined such an unfree state, in a futuristic novel called *1984*. Orwell's state, which is forever at war, is ruled by a dictator known as Big Brother. This still from the 1956 movie of the book shows how the people are under constant surveillance by Big Brother's listening and viewing devices.

TAKING PART

Citizens from the state of Florida dispute the way in which votes were counted during the 2000 United States presidential election. If democracy is to work, then all citizens must be allowed to vote and prepared to take part. The system must be fair and deliver what it promises. People will only bother to vote if they believe that they really can influence policy or bring about change.

Democratic roots

WHEN PREHISTORIC PEOPLE hunted and gathered, government was not really necessary. As populations grew and cities developed, rulers emerged to organize society. Sometimes their power was balanced by councils of important people. Parts of ancient Iraq and India had citizens' assemblies. A new system of government by the people arose in Greece from 508 BCE. It was called *demokratia*, from *demos* ("people") and *kratía* ("rule"). This was direct democracy—citizens came to the assembly and voted for themselves on all major issues.

DAWN OF DEMOCRACY
The rocks in the foreground of this picture are part of the Pnyx, the hill in Athens where, from the sixth century BCE, a public assembly called the Ekklesia met. The citizens who made up the Ekklesia elected new officials and debated public policies, such as going to war. Athens was one of several independent city-states that made up ancient Greece, and it was the first to try democracy.

Wreath, a symbol of victory, is placed on the head of demos (the "people")

Demokratia is shown as a goddess

DEMOCRACY OR TYRANNY?
The Greeks loved to argue about politics. They tried monarchy (rule by a king), tyranny (rule by a strong leader or "tyrant"), and oligarchy (rule by a few powerful people). This pillar from around 337 BCE proclaims a law against tyranny. Supporters of tyranny believed that a leader would rule more wisely than the people.

Details of the law are carved in marble and displayed for all to see

WHO COULD VOTE?
In Athens, voting was open to male citizens, but not to women, foreign residents, or slaves. Assembly attendance was generally about 5,000. Citizens who failed to attend were publicly shamed, being lashed with ropes covered in red dye.

Bronze voting token from ancient Athens

Battle helmet symbolizes Perikles' victories in war

Toga's broad, purple stripe indicates rank of senator

THE AGE OF PERIKLES

Perikles, a powerful statesman and general, led Athens from 461 to 429 BCE, thanks to his powerful skills of oratory (public speaking) and rhetoric (persuasion). After his death, Athenian democracy survived for about a century. Then, in 338 BCE, the city-state was defeated by King Philip II of Macedonia.

Hippokrates, of the powerful Alkmeonid family

Pottery fragment

OSTRACIZED!

If citizens of Athens agreed that a politician was causing trouble or trying to seize power, they could vote for him to be exiled for ten years. Proposed names were scratched on fragments of pottery, called *ostraka*. We still talk about people being "ostracized" if they are excluded from society.

Speaker had to finish before all the water trickled out through this hole

Restored klepsydra made from earthenware

CITIZENS SPEAK OUT

This water clock or *klepsydra* was used to time speeches in the Athenian law courts, or Dikasteria. It helped people keep their arguments short and to the point. Like the Ekklesia and Boule (the popular council that ran Athens from day to day), the law courts were democratic; cases were heard not by judges but by elected citizens.

REPUBLICAN ROME

The ancient Romans abolished monarchy in 509 BCE and founded a republic (from *res publica*, meaning "the public matter"). This was governed by several separate assemblies, with elected officials called magistrates. Assembly membership depended on class, family, and income. It was not open to women, slaves, or non-Romans. The most important assembly was the senate, made up of upper-class Romans called patricians. Lower-class citizens were known as plebeians.

Fasces, symbol of rule

Eagle, symbol of Rome

Laurel wreath, symbol of glory

SPQR

These letters stand for *senatus populusque Romanus*, which means "the senate and the people of Rome." Their appearance on Roman coins, decrees, and battle standards made it clear that the authority of Roman government depended on the people, not just the senate. In the later years of the republic, the plebeians became more and more powerful.

IMPERIAL ROME

During the first century BCE the political ideals of the Roman republic began to crumble. Sweeping powers were given to the general Julius Caesar and then to his successor Octavian, who ruled as the emperor Augustus from 27 BCE to 14 CE. In this altar frieze made for Augustus, senators and public officials appear together in a procession. Under Augustus and later emperors, however, the power of the senate soon declined.

Senator

Veiled high priest

Ara Pacis, funeral altar built to honor Augustus

Lictors (public officials)

The first parliaments

ROME FELL TO INVADERS IN 476 CE. The thousand years that followed are known as the Middle Ages. Across Europe, these were times of warfare and hardship, with few rights for the common people. However, some modern parliaments can trace their origins to this period. In Scandinavia, Viking chieftains and free men used to meet at public assemblies to vote for new laws and settle disputes. Iceland's parliament, the Althing, was originally founded by Vikings in 930 CE. Most medieval realms were monarchies, in which kings governed and administered justice in alliance with landowning nobles.

Lewis chess set

ALL THE KING'S MEN
This chess set, which is about 850 years old, shows the structure of medieval society. Kings were the most powerful players. However, from the 1200s, royal power was challenged by the church, by nobles, and later by merchants in the cities. To agree on new laws, kings had to summon councils of important people. These were called parliaments, meaning "talking sessions."

WITANAGEMOT
An 11th-century manuscript painting represents one of the Anglo-Saxon kings who ruled England at that time. He is surrounded by the witenagemot ("council of the wise"), made up of powerful nobles, or witans. Nobles were not just advisors—they had the power to decide who succeeded the king.

A witan or councilor

King carries symbols of royal authority—crown, sword, and scepter

FRENCH PARLIAMENT
A French parliament meets to depose King Henry III in 1589. Parliaments were summoned in many lands, including France, Spain, Portugal, Poland, England, and Scotland. They were not yet democratic assemblies, as membership was limited to the most powerful social classes or "estates."

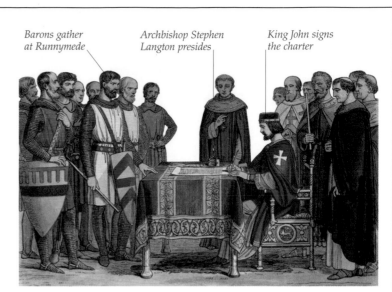

Barons gather at Runnymede

Archbishop Stephen Langton presides

King John signs the charter

MAGNA CARTA
In 1215, English barons (powerful lords) forced King John (r. 1199–1216) to sign a *Magna Carta*, or "Great Charter," that guaranteed citizens of England certain rights. It confirmed that even kings are subject to the law of the land. The charter was reissued over the next 500 years and is still seen as an important milestone on the road to democracy.

A criminal is hanged, to show that justice (as well as law-making, taxes, defense, and foreign affairs) was determined through debate by councilors

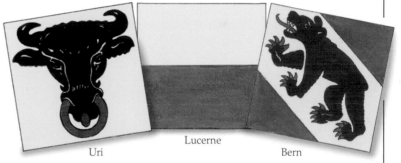

Uri
Lucerne
Bern

SWISS CANTONS
These flags represent three of the small states, or cantons, that came together to form Switzerland in 1291. In contrast to the many European states ruled by monarchs in the Middle Ages, the Swiss cantons developed more democratic forms of government, including elected city councils and popular assemblies.

VENICE VOTES
This is the Great Council Chamber in Venice, Italy. Venice was a republic, ruled by various councils who elected a leader, or doge. At first there was a broad franchise, but after 1297, voting was greatly restricted. By the 1500s, the council's 2,500 members all came from a handful of Venice's leading families.

THE KING IS DEAD
Charles I was beheaded in London in January 1649, on the orders of Parliament. A Roman law against tyranny was used to justify his death. The execution shocked all of Europe. Most people believed that kings had a God-given right to rule. To the end, Charles insisted that the people should have no part in government.

Charles I is blessed by a priest before his execution

Silk undershirt worn by Charles I at his execution

The world "turned upside down"

SOME EARLY PARLIAMENTS ALLOWED NON-NOBLES to take part, as representatives from the growing towns. In England this "estate," known as the Commons, became more and more powerful. In the 1620s King Charles I, determined to uphold royal authority, repeatedly clashed with Parliament. A civil war (1642–1651) broke out between the two sides. In the words of a popular song of 1643, it was as if the world was being "turned upside down." Parliament declared a republic or Commonwealth in 1649, and ruled through a Council of State.

OLIVER CROMWELL
In 1653 Oliver Cromwell took power as "Lord Protector." Cromwell died in 1658, and his successor was not such an able ruler. In 1660 Parliament voted to restore the monarchy and Charles II was crowned king.

Leveller presents demands to Parliament, 1647

HOPES CRUSHED
Cromwell's supporters included rich landowners and merchants. Many poor workers backed a group of radicals known as the Levellers, who demanded democratic rights for all. The movement was quickly crushed under the Commonwealth.

Charles I wore another shirt over this one as he did want to be seen shivering—in case people thought he was afraid

JACOBITE RISINGS
Charles II's son, James II, was forced into exile in 1688, in a "Glorious Revolution." His supporters, the Jacobites, tried to regain the throne, but were finally defeated in 1746.

WILLIAM AND MARY
From 1689 England was ruled by William III and Mary II. They agreed to a Bill of Rights, which set out rights for the people and made it clear that monarchs reigned only by consent of the people, as represented in Parliament.

After consenting to the Bill of Rights, William and Mary are presented with the crown

NUMBER TEN
The door to London's 10 Downing Street is the most famous door in Britain. In the 1720s, government affairs became increasingly taken over by the king's chief or "prime" minister. From 1731, Number 10 was his official residence.

NEW POLITICS IN BRITAIN
Philosophers added to political debate in these stormy years. Thomas Hobbes (1588–1679) believed that humans, acting in self-interest, needed to agree to strong government. John Locke (1632–1704) believed in human reason and the right to rebel. From the 1680s there were two political parties. Whigs supported the Bill of Rights, while Tories were conservative royalists. Elections were often corrupt—William Hogarth satirized them in the 1750s in a series of paintings, such as this one, *The Polling*.

The coachmen ignore the problem and play cards

The coach of Britannia, representing the nation, has broken down

The dying, the sick, and the insane are dragged to the polling station

Candidates, officials, and supporters are asleep or drunk

A disabled soldier tries to take the oath by placing his hook on the Bible

Lawyers argue whether the oath is valid

Revolution in North America

IN THE 1600S AND 1700S Europe's most powerful nations were building overseas empires. By 1763 Britain ruled 13 colonies in North America, between the east coast and the Mississippi River. Many of the people who had settled there were religious and political dissidents. They objected to the British government's control of trade and taxation. Inspired by new ideas about the rights of man, they also campaigned for the vote. Why should they pay taxes to a government in which they were not represented? The British government, fearful that ideas of liberty would spread back home, struggled to keep control as a full-scale revolution broke out across the Atlantic Ocean.

BOSTON TEA PARTY
Britain began to impose taxes on its North American colonies in 1765. They were strongly resisted. Taxes on tea—and unfair trade in tea—were especially resented. In December 1773, rebels disguised as American Indians boarded a British ship in the harbor at Boston, Massachusetts, and threw its precious cargo of 46 tons of tea overboard.

FLYING THE FLAG
Flags mark America's transition from a group of colonies to an independent nation, the United States. As states joined the union in the 19th century, more and more stars were added to the flag. The American Revolution inspired freedom struggles in Europe and South America.

DECLARATION OF INDEPENDENCE
On July 4, 1776, the American colonies issued a Declaration of Independence. It was mostly written by Thomas Jefferson and contained the revolutionary line, "All men are created equal." It also spoke of people's right to "Life, Liberty and the Pursuit of Happiness."

GEORGE WASHINGTON
It was General Washington who led the rebel troops against the British and won the Revolutionary War. The new United States introduced a system of presidential democracy and Washington served as first president of the new nation from 1789 to 1797.

LIBERTY BELL

This famous bell, now cracked, is in Philadelphia, but there are copies across the United States. It was rung in 1774 to mark the First Continental Congress (a meeting of representatives from all the American colonies). It was rung in 1775 to mark the first battles of the war, and it may have rung in 1776 at the Declaration of Independence.

Crack is 24½ in (60 cm) long

Inscription reads, "Proclaim liberty throughout all the land and to all the inhabitants thereof"

AMERICAN REVOLUTION (1775–1781)

The creation of a new democracy in America could not be achieved without a war against the British and their loyalist supporters. The Revolutionary War ended with the British surrender (reenacted above) at Yorktown in 1781.

THE RIGHTS OF MAN

Thomas Paine (1737–1809) took part in the American and French revolutions. He opposed monarchy and campaigned for human rights, a new idea at the time. He wrote *The Rights of Man* (1791).

George Washington, first president 1789–1797

Thomas Jefferson, third president 1801–1809

Abraham Lincoln, 16th president 1861–1865

Theodore Roosevelt, 26th president 1901–1909

MOUNT RUSHMORE

From 1927, gigantic heads of four US presidents were carved into Mount Rushmore, South Dakota. The monument was intended as a shrine to democracy, but for years the new republic had not extended democratic equality to women, African Americans, or American Indians.

Supreme Court

Library of Congress

Senate is in north wing of Capitol building

Tea

Tea

CAPITOL HILL

The United States today is a federal nation, in which states still make their own laws. The national legislature is on Capitol Hill in the federal capital, Washington, DC. It is made up of a Senate and a House of Representatives.

House of Representatives is in south wing of Capitol building

France in turmoil

FRANCE IN 1789 was in a deep political crisis. The monarchy had enjoyed absolute power during the long reign of Louis XIV, which lasted from 1643 to 1715. The nobles and the clergy still enjoyed special privileges, which held back the rise of the middle classes—merchants, doctors, and lawyers. Farm laborers and city workers were desperately poor and often starved. Taxation was high, in order to pay for endless wars. Arguments about voting rights had already set off revolutions in Britain and America. Now they triggered a violent social upheaval in France as well. The French revolutionaries tried to bring in democracy by drastic social change, but they became bitterly divided among themselves and ended up ruling by terror.

JEAN-JACQUES ROUSSEAU
The 1700s were a time of new ideas in France. Thinkers became more interested in science and reason than in religious faith. Jean-Jacques Rousseau (1712–1778) who influenced many revolutionaries, attacked social inequality and argued that laws must be made by an assembly of the people.

THE SANS-CULOTTES
Sans culottes means "without breeches." It was a nickname for the working men of Paris, who wore long trousers rather than the knee-length breeches of the middle and upper classes. The Parisian mob, which included men and women, was armed and violent. Their anger was whipped up by politicians. After the revolution in France, other European governments came to fear the common people.

Costume of a sans-culotte

Republican cockade (hat badge)

Red cap of liberty (based on cap worn by ancient Greek slaves)

Carmagnole, a short jacket

Sash in the republican colors

FASHIONS FOR CITIZENS
By 1793 even French wallpaper had a revolutionary design. The traditional colors of France (red, white, and blue) now stood for the values of the revolution—Liberty, Equality, and Fraternity (brotherhood). People addressed each other as "citizen" and adopted customs of the Roman republic. A new calendar was introduced, in which 1792 became Year I of the Republic, and religious festivals were abolished.

Tricolor (three colors) of red, white, and blue

RF stands for République Française (the French Republic)

The virtue of union

Jean-Jacques Rousseau

The virtue of justice

The virtue of force (strength)

A PACK OF CARDS

From 1792 the use of all royal emblems was banned. Even packs of playing cards were redesigned to be more republican. The jack, queen, and king were replaced by figures that represented ideal virtues and values, such as prosperity or justice, or by famous citizens such as Jean-Jacques Rousseau.

Pantalon (long trousers) instead of tailored breeches

Leather, buckled shoe (but most sans-culottes wore plain, wooden clogs called sabots).

NAPOLEON

From 1795 a new form of government was introduced, called the Directory. In 1799 a *coup d'état* (seizure of power) was led by a young soldier called Napoleon Bonaparte. In 1804 he was crowned emperor. A form of monarchy had returned, but the democratic ideals of Liberty, Equality, and Fraternity did live on.

This painting by Jacques-Louis David records the meeting in 1789 at which members of France's Commons swore to create a democratic National Assembly. They had just been locked out of a meeting at the palace of Versailles. The Commons represented the mass of the people but in the French assembly, or Estates-General, they could easily be outvoted by the nobles and clergy.

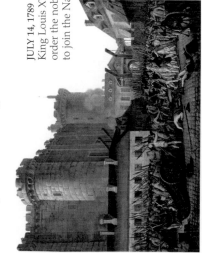

JULY 14, 1789

King Louis XVI was forced to order the nobles and clergy to join the National Assembly. However, when he fired a finance minister who supported reform and moved troops into Paris, protesters filled the streets. They seized arms and stormed the Bastille, a fortress used as a royal prison.

THE KING EXECUTED

The revolution was made up of many different factions, moderate and extreme. It had many enemies, both inside and outside France. A frenzy of killing broke out on the streets of Paris. In 1792 the monarchy was abolished and in 1793 King Louis XVI was executed by guillotine.

ROBESPIERRE AND THE TERROR

Maximilien Robespierre (1758–1794) was a member of a radical political faction called the Jacobins. He was a leader during the Reign of Terror (1793–1794), a period in which thousands of nobles and political rivals were executed. In the end he too was beheaded by guillotine. The ideals of democracy had become soaked in blood.

Slaves or citizens?

In the 1780s and 1790s, there was much talk of democracy, liberty, and human rights. Yet slavery, the exact opposite of these ideals, still existed in many parts of the world. The wealth of Europe and the Americas depended on a shameful trade in African slaves, who were forced to work on plantations growing sugar cane and cotton. Ever since the first democracy in Athens, slaves had been denied the right to vote or to be represented. Would they now be treated as equals?

BREAKING FREE
Slaves sometimes fought for their freedom. These slaves break free during a voyage and attack the traders who have made their lives a misery. There were also revolts and rebellions in the Caribbean. A few slaves succeeded in escaping to remote countryside or small islands. But most could only dream of a better world in which they shared equal rights.

Iron bars made it impossible for the wearer to move freely or associate with others

IN CHAINS
This spiked iron collar was put on the necks of slaves who tried to run away or who refused to submit to the will of their "owners." Slaves were often beaten and separated from their families. No country that allowed such treatment could claim to be a land of freedom.

SLAVE SHIPS
These drawings show how African slaves crossed the Atlantic Ocean, packed on board ships like cattle. They were chained by the hands and feet. Many died on the voyage and were thrown overboard. On arrival in the Americas, the slaves were sold at auction. Between 1540 and 1850, as many as 15 million Africans were transported on ships like these.

Padlock

Slaves wore only a loincloth

Pottery medallion manufactured
by Josiah Wedgwood in 1786

*Antislavery
motto*

*Cameo shows a
kneeling African
slave in chains*

A MAN AND A BROTHER
This medallion became the emblem
of Britain's antislavery movement.
Slavery was illegal in Britain from
1772 but continued in Britain's
overseas empire. Campaigners
who fought to ban it included
Member of Parliament
William Wilberforce
(1759–1833). Slavery
in the empire was
finally abolished
in 1833.

HARRIET TUBMAN
In the United States, some
revolutionaries, such as
Thomas Paine, opposed
slavery, while others, such
as George Washington, were
slave owners. By 1804 slavery
had been banned in the
northern states, but it continued
in the South. Harriet Tubman
(c. 1822–1913), an escaped slave,
helped many others to flee from the
South to Canada, via a secret route
known as the "underground railroad."

THE AMERICAN CIVIL WAR
Between 1861 and 1865 a bitter
civil war was fought between the
Union forces of the northern
states and the Confederate
forces of the South. Slavery
was opposed by President
Abraham Lincoln, but still
practiced in the South. It was
finally abolished throughout
the United States in 1865.

Hat worn for
formal occasions by a Union
officer in the American Civil War

Black cockade (rosette)

*Collar
fastening
could lock shut*

A regiment of free African
Americans fights for the Union

TOUSSAINT!
Toussaint L'Ouverture
(1743–1803) was a
freed slave from the French
colony of Haiti in the
Caribbean. He joined
rebel slaves, fought
European armies, and
became Haiti's virtual ruler.
However, French troops under
Napoleon took Toussaint captive
and he died in prison. France did
not abolish slavery until 1848.

THE RIGHT TO VOTE
Although slavery had been abolished in
the United States, many states passed laws
known as Black Codes that limited the civil
rights of former slaves. At last, in 1870,
changes were made to the US Constitution to
ensure that no citizen's right to vote could be
refused or limited on account of race, color,
or previous status as a slave. The struggle for
equality, however, was not yet over.

Power to the workers

THE 1800S SAW THE BIRTH of the industrial age. With the invention of powered machines, it became possible to mass-produce goods cheaply and then ship them around the world. The people who had the money to invest in these businesses made their fortunes. However, the men, women, and children who actually worked in the mills and factories received very low wages. Life in the big, new cities was often unhealthy and wretched. Poor people still had no vote and no say in how society should be governed.

THE FACTORY AGE
Industrial development began in Britain in the 1700s. In the 1800s it spread through northern Europe and the northeastern United States. In many countries, political systems had changed little since the Middle Ages. There was pressing need for change and for social justice.

Rebel holds white flag of surrender

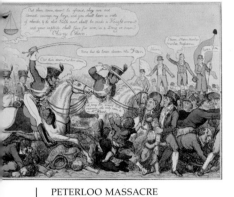

PETERLOO MASSACRE
This cartoon shows the events of the Peterloo Massacre (named after the famous battle of Waterloo) of 1819. Thousands of protesters gathered on St. Peter's Fields in the industrial city of Manchester, England, to demand votes for all citizens. Charged by mounted troops, at least 11 people were killed and 500 injured.

VOTING REFORM
The secret ballot was introduced to Britain in 1872. It was one of several reforms called for in the 1830s and 1840s by campaigners called Chartists. Their *People's Charter* demanded votes for all men over 21, fair electoral districts, and payment for Members of Parliament (so that Parliament was open to everyone, not just the rich).

Workers were demanding better wages, better working conditions, and political representation

Strike leaders wear the same simple working clothes as the other laborers behind them

Fiumana (A Flood) by Giuseppe Pellizza da Volpedo, 1896

REVOLUTIONS OF 1848
Revolts broke out in Frankfurt in September 1848. Plans to create a united, democratic Germany with a broad franchise failed, in the face of international opposition and internal divisions. The same year saw revolutions in dozens of European cities.

BADGE OF A COMMUNARD
For two months in 1871, after France's defeat by Prussia, the Paris city council or commune set up its own government. Elected delegates introduced a new kind of democracy, open to working people and even women. However, the French government recaptured Paris and executed thousands of the rebels.

Medal of the Paris Commune— "Liberty, Equality, Fraternity"

Friedrich Engels (1820–1895)

Karl Marx (1818–1883)

REVOLUTION, NOT REFORM
German thinkers Karl Marx and Friedrich Engels believed that democracy could never develop in an unjust society. First, a classless or communist society must be created. Workers had to seize control of production from the factory owners and capitalists.

CAPITALIST INVESTORS
Political power was held by men like the ones in this 1887 painting by Ferencz Paczka. They had capital (money) to invest in companies, and any profits went to them rather than to the workers who made the goods.

MARCH OF THE COMMON PEOPLE
In this painting of 1896, Italian workers go on strike. By withholding their labor and forming trade unions, the poorest people in society found that they could exert some power after all. In the 19th century, political argument raged among conservative and liberal capitalists, among socialists and communists who supported the working classes, and among anarchists who opposed the authority of the state.

Women play an ever more important part in politics

GIUSEPPE GARIBALDI (1807–1882)
Garibaldi was an Italian freedom fighter who helped to unite Italy, and became a popular hero around the world. In 1879 he founded the League of Democracy, to promote universal suffrage—votes for all.

Double-headed eagle, emblem
of the vast Russian empire

Empire and freedom

MANY PEOPLE IN 19TH-CENTURY EUROPE were struggling to win the vote or to create a society in which democracy could exist. In European countries' overseas empires, self-government was only given to people of European descent. African, Asian, Caribbean, and Pacific nationalists began to campaign for their own representation and independence. In some colonies, legislative (law-making) councils were eventually formed, with limited powers. When colonies at last won their freedom in the second half of the 20th century, many were able to sustain democratic government—but others were not.

GLOBAL EMPIRE
This map of 1886 shows the British empire. By 1921 it governed one quarter of all the people in the world. Other large empires were governed by France, Germany, the Netherlands, Belgium, Portugal, and Spain. Empires provided Europe with raw materials for industry, cheap labor, and new markets for goods. Slavery had been abolished, but for most colonial peoples there was still little chance of fair wages, political freedom, or democracy.

Shipping carries colonial produce around the world

Pink shows extent of British rule

Sailor represents naval power

Indian laborer performs backbreaking work

Military power gives Europeans dominance

Happy "natives" reap the rewards of empire

Britannia sits on top of the world, resting her arm on a Union Jack shield

SOUTH AMERICAN HOPES

This painting shows freedom fighter Simón Bolívar at the Battle of Carabobo (1821), where he won Venezuelan independence. Bolívar freed much of South America from the Spanish. However, powerful landowners and generals thwarted early hopes for new democratic governments on the continent.

NEW PARLIAMENTS

At this conference in London in 1866, Canada was made a Dominion within the British empire. Australia became a Commonwealth in 1901 and New Zealand a Dominion in 1907. These changes created new nations that shared a constitutional monarch with Britain, but developed lively, independent parliamentary democracies of their own.

NO FREEDOM IN AFRICA

In this photograph from 1895, the Herero people of southwest Africa (modern Namibia) sign a treaty with the German colonial commander. The harsh treatment of the African population by the whites led to an uprising nine years later, which was put down with the loss of as many as 75,000 lives.

Aboriginal woman and kangaroo represent Australia

White settlers are granted self-rule

White Kenyan police officer guards Kikuyu men, suspected of taking part in the Mau Mau rebellion

Kikuyu people had been forced to give up their farmland to white settlers

STIRRINGS OF LIBERTY

European settlers in Kenya were given a legislative council in 1907, but Africans could not be elected to it until 1957. Violence had broken out from 1952 onward, during the so-called Mau Mau rebellion. Kenya finally won its independence from Britain in 1963. However from 1966 to 1991 it was a one-party state, in which no opposition party was allowed to run for election.

YEARS OF INDEPENDENCE

The new nations faced problems. The colonial period had often stirred up trouble between ethnic groups, and failed to educate the population or build a strong economy. Corruption and rule by dictators became common. Despite the difficulties, however, democracies flourished in many new lands, from India to the Caribbean.

Flag of independent Jamaica, 1962

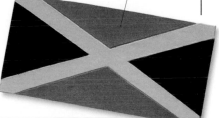

Votes for women

WOMEN HAD RULED AS MONARCHS or been influential behind the scenes, but they had never been given the vote in ancient or medieval assemblies. By the 1800s some women were being allowed to vote in regional or state elections. But national elections were not open to females until 1893, when women in New Zealand at last gained the vote. Finland followed in 1905. Women in Switzerland did not win the vote until 1971 and in Liechtenstein until 1984. In a few countries around the world, women still do not have the right to vote.

FIRST TO THE POLLS
This bronze memorial, erected in Christchurch in 1993, commemorates 100 years of women's suffrage in New Zealand. It is named after Kate Sheppard (1848–1934), a leading campaigner who collected tens of thousands of signatures in support of women's votes. After success in 1893, Sheppard went on to fight for further voting reforms, such as proportional representation, which takes into account all votes cast.

Kate Sheppard National Memorial, New Zealand

MUMMY'S A SUFFRAGETTE
In Britain the campaign for women's suffrage (right to vote) began in the 1830s. In 1887 the National Union of Women's Suffrage Societies (NUWSS) was founded. Later campaigners (called suffragettes) favored militant tactics. They were derided in posters like this one for neglecting their duties as mothers.

Mummy's a Suffragette

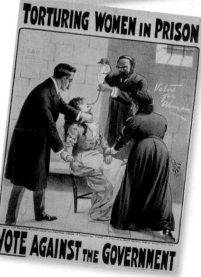

Police officer carries Emmeline Pankhurst away from a protest, 1914

HUNGER STRIKES AND FORCE FEEDING
When protesting suffragettes broke the law in Britain, they were imprisoned. After 1909, many went on hunger strike and were force-fed through tubes by the prison authorities. This was a brutal process that may have resulted in the deaths of some women.

LAW AND ORDER
Emmeline Pankhurst (1857–1928) founded the radical Women's Social and Political Union (WSPU) in 1903. The suffragettes smashed windows and set fire to buildings. One of them, Emily Wilding Davison, threw herself in front of the king's horse at a famous horse race, and was killed.

THE WOMEN'S SUFFRAGE GAME

This board game was produced by Britain's WSPU in 1909 and was called Pank-a-Squith (after Emmeline Pankhurst and the prime minister, Herbert Asquith). It shows scenes from the suffragettes' battles with the government. World War I (1914–1918) was a turning point for the suffragettes. Many women took over men's jobs, and this changed how society saw them. Women over 30 were given the vote in 1918. All men and women over 21 received the vote in 1929.

A newly invented airplane proclaims "VOTES FOR WOMEN"

Holloway Prison, London, where many suffragettes were jailed

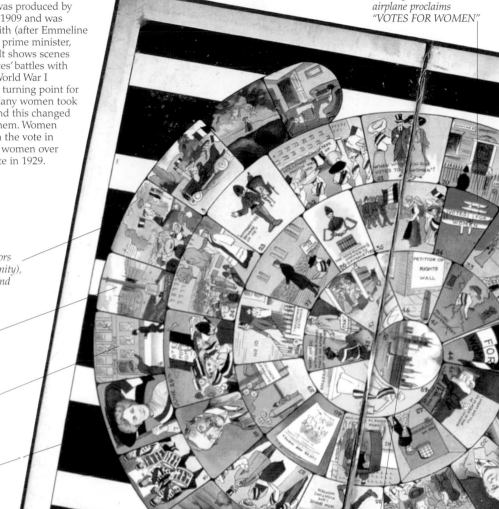

The suffragettes' colors were purple (for dignity), white (for purity), and green (for hope)

Suffragettes hold a political rally in Trafalgar Square, London

Suffragettes break windows of government buildings

Emmeline Pankhurst, founder of the WSPU

Goal of the game (and of the suffragettes) is to reach the Houses of Parliament

Buttons from the US campaign for women's suffrage

Herbert Asquith, UK prime minister 1908–1916

Sirimavo Bandaranaike, the world's first female prime minister

AMERICAN SISTERS

In the United States, the struggle for women's right to vote grew up alongside the antislavery campaign. An escaped slave named Sojourner Truth (c. 1797–1883) was an eloquent speaker for women's rights. In 1868 Elizabeth Cady Stanton (1815–1902) and Susan B. Anthony (1820–1906) founded the American Equal Rights Association. It was 1920 before the US constitution was changed to give women the federal vote.

WOMEN IN CHARGE

The next struggle faced by women was to be accepted as candidates in national elections, and to serve as members of parliament. The first woman in the world to be elected as prime minister was Sirimavo Bandaranaike (1916–2000) of Ceylon (now Sri Lanka), in 1960.

Red revolution

From 1914 to 1918, the terrible conflict of World War I engulfed the world's empires, monarchies, and republics and killed more than 13.5 million men. In the 1920s and '30s there followed economic chaos, in which rich people lost their fortunes and working people their jobs. Many looked to political theories such as Marxism (see page 23) for explanations and solutions. Social democratic parties tried to reform society and make it fairer, while revolutionary communists (or "Reds") attempted to overthrow capitalism altogether and replace it with a centrally planned economy. By contrast to liberal democracies, in "people's democracies" only Communist Party candidates could stand for election. Communists claimed that the party was the true representative of the working class.

OCTOBER REVOLUTION
Russia created a Duma or parliament in 1905, but it had no powers. In February 1917 (March, by the modern calendar), a revolution overthrew the Russian czar or emperor. The new government was short-lived. Public anger about economic problems and Russia's role in World War I helped a party of Marxist revolutionaries called the Bolsheviks seize power in October (November) 1917.

WORLDWIDE ACTION
Women members of the Industrial Workers of the World (IWW), or "Wobblies," march in New York City in 1913. Members of the organization included trade unionists, socialists, communists, and anarchists.

LENIN AND THE BOLSHEVIKS
Vladimir Lenin (1870–1924) was leader of the communist Bolsheviks. Like Marx, he rejected liberal democracy and reform. He believed that the only just society would be run by the workers. A centrally controlled Communist Party was to lead the way in bringing this about.

VOTING FOR THE PARTY
By 1928 Joseph Stalin (1878–1953) had gained control over Soviet Russia. Here he casts his vote in Moscow in 1937. Although everyone could vote under Stalin, candidates were chosen by the Communist Party leadership and elected unopposed. Stalin effectively ruled as dictator.

IDEALS CRUSHED
This statuette shows a woman sewing a communist banner. Under Stalin, many of Russia's original idealists and revolutionaries were murdered by secret police, put on trial, or sent to grim labor camps.

THE SOVIETS

The revolutionaries' model of democracy was based on elected workers' committees called soviets. Each soviet elected representatives up to the highest level. From 1922 to 1991 Russia was part of what was known as the Union of Soviet Socialist Republics (or Soviet Union).

Red Army badge of 1919 shows a hammer and plow

Soviet badge shows a hammer (representing industrial workers) and sickle (representing peasant farmers)

THE RED ARMY

After 1917 the former Russian empire was the scene of a desperate civil war between the communist Red Army, led by Leon Trotsky, and the imperialist "Whites," supported by forces from other countries. By 1922 the Red Army controlled Russia.

Bolshevik identified by red armband

Postcard showing the October Revolution

THE COLD WAR YEARS

Huge missiles are paraded in Moscow in 1962. During World War II (1939–1945) the Soviet Union was allied with the liberal democracies of the West. However, from 1945 until 1990 there was a terrifying arms race and a period of international tension known as the Cold War. On the one side were the United States and its allies. On the other side were the world's growing number of Communist governments.

COMMUNISM IN CHINA

Chinese communists came to power in 1949 and created a one-party state. Land was given over to peasants. Progress was made in education and housing, but industrial reforms were disastrous and millions starved. A portrait of Communist leader Mao Zedong (1893–1976) still appears on Beijing's Imperial Palace (right), but since his death the Chinese Communist Party has moved toward a market economy under state direction.

THE BERLIN WALL

After World War II, the German city of Berlin was divided into two zones—the communist East and the capitalist West. In 1961, a wall was built to prevent people from fleeing from the East. Its demolition by crowds in 1989 marked the last phase of the Cold War. The Soviet Union collapsed in 1991.

THE LITTLE RED BOOK

About 900 million copies of this small book have been printed since 1964. It contains the thoughts of Mao Zedong on "revolutionary democracy." For many years, everyone in China was expected to read it. Like Stalin, Mao was publicly glorified while he was in power—just as emperors were in earlier times.

Fascists on the march

IL DUCE
Known as *Il Duce*, "the Leader," Benito Mussolini (1883–1945) directed the Italian fascist movement from 1919. He manipulated the voting system in his favor and intimidated voters. He played on fears of communism and gained power with the backing of leading industrialists.

THE END OF WORLD WAR I in 1918 did not bring peace to the world, but bitterness, political violence, and economic problems. Governments came under attack from new political movements that opposed all kinds of democracy, whether liberal or revolutionary. The Italian fascists took their name from the *fasces*—bundles of rods and axes that had symbolized state authority in ancient Rome. A "Nazi" (National Socialist) Party was founded in Germany in 1920, and similar parties were formed in many other countries. They glorified dictatorship, the state, and war. Many were racist. They suppressed the rights of individuals, and although they sometimes used votes as a means of gaining power, they preferred to use bullying and violence.

German children play with worthless banknotes in 1923

A CLIMATE OF FEAR
After losing World War I, Germany was forced to pay large sums of money as reparations, and was also hit by the world economic crisis. Money had no value because of soaring prices. Democratic government was weakened, and the Nazis began to win support.

ROAD TO WAR
Germany had been barred from rearming after World War I, but Nazi leader Adolf Hitler built up the German army. From 1938 he began to expand the German empire by invading Austria and Czechoslovakia. Britain and France declared war on Germany in 1939. During World War II (1939–1945), Germany was allied with Italy and Japan.

Soldiers march under Nazi standards in Nuremberg, Germany, in September 1933

THE NAZI SWASTIKA
The ancient symbol of the swastika was adopted as the badge of the German Nazi Party. At first the Nazis made use of the democratic system to win votes, aided by propaganda, lies, and thuggery against their opponents. By 1933 the Nazis were in control, able to create a brutal dictatorship and suppress democracy.

THE FÜHRER
Austrian-born Adolf Hitler (1889–1945) was known as the *Führer*, "the Leader," of the Nazis. He believed that democratic government was the "rule of stupidity, of mediocrity."

MARK OF A JEW
In Germany, and then in the countries that they occupied, the Nazis forced Jews to wear yellow stars. The Nazis murdered 6 million Jews. They also killed Roma, Slavs, disabled people, homosexuals, and political opponents.

Dutch word for "Jew"

THE FIGHT AGAINST FASCISM
The Spanish Civil War was fought from 1936 to 1939. Spain's democratic republican government was supported by volunteers from around the world. They were defeated by fascists, nationalists, and conservatives led by General Francisco Franco.

TODAY'S NAZIS
By 1945 World War II had ended with the deaths of Mussolini and Hitler and the defeat of the militarist government of Japan. Extreme nationalism, fascism, and racism are still pursued by some political parties around the world, but most of these groups remain very small.

Regardless of color

Sɪɴᴄᴇ ᴛʜᴇ ᴅᴀʏs ᴏғ ᴀɴᴄɪᴇɴᴛ Aᴛʜᴇɴs, voting and political rights have been tied to ethnicity or race. In the 1930s, the Nazis in Germany began by denying Jews the right to vote and ended up by denying them the right to live. In 1948 the South African government denied its black and Asian populations any voting rights, as part of a system of racial segregation (keeping people from different races apart) known in the Afrikaans language as apartheid. In the United States, African Americans faced an ongoing political struggle through the 1940s, '50s, and '60s to gain civil rights—basic citizens' rights. The Voting Rights Act of 1965 was passed to make sure that their right to vote, won in 1870, was actually enforced. Many of the greatest battles for the franchise or right to vote have been fighting racist restrictions.

OLYMPIC PROTEST
At the 1968 Olympic Games in Mexico City, American medal winners in the 200 meters event, Tommie Smith and John Carlos, raised their fists in a "black power" salute. African Americans were demanding social and economic justice as well as civil rights.

MARTIN LUTHER KING DREAMS OF JUSTICE
Civil rights activist Dr. Martin Luther King Jr. (1929–1968) addressed a 300,000-strong protest march in Washington, DC in 1963. "We can never be satisfied," he declared, "as long as a Negro in Mississippi cannot vote and a Negro in New York believes he has nothing for which to vote." King was assassinated in Memphis, Tennessee, in 1968.

AMERICAN BUS BOYCOTT

African American Rosa Parks sits on board a bus in Montgomery, Alabama. In 1955 Parks was arrested and fined for refusing to give up her seat to a white man. In response, the National Association for the Advancement of Colored People (NAACP) organized a boycott of the city's buses until segregation laws were lifted. At that time, black people in some southern states were forced to eat apart from whites in restaurants, and to send their children to different schools. All kinds of methods were devised to prevent blacks from voting.

FLYING THE ABORIGINAL FLAG

Aboriginal Australians had to campaign hard for the same rights as other Australians, even though they had lived in Australia for about 50,000 years. Like other Australians, they became citizens in 1948, but it was left to individual states to grant them the vote in state elections. Finally, in 1967, a new law formally included Aboriginals in the Australian political community as equals.

Bronze sculpture of
Nelson Mandela
(b. 1918)

APARTHEID IN SOUTH AFRICA

In Africa, the descendants of some white settlers refused to hand over democratic powers to the black African majority. This led to war in Rhodesia (now Zimbabwe) and to terrible oppression in South Africa. Nelson Mandela of the African National Congress (ANC), a leading campaigner against the apartheid system, was imprisoned for 28 years—and his party was banned. Mandela's release in 1990 marked the collapse of apartheid.

VOTES FOR ALL

Africans in the Transkei, a region of South Africa, line up to cast their votes in the historic general election of 1994. It was the first time that blacks in South Africa had been allowed to vote. Under the leadership of Nelson Mandela, the ANC won 62 percent of the vote. Mandela served as South Africa's first black president from 1994 to 1999.

MULTIETHNIC AUSTRALIA

Australia's 1988 parliament building in Canberra is fronted by a mosaic that honors the Aboriginal people. Today, Australian voters come from many ethnic backgrounds.

Modern struggles

OVER THE LAST CENTURY, the right to vote has been extended to many social groups and populations that were previously unrepresented. However, struggles for human and civil rights continue in many parts of the world. Some countries are ruled by oppressive or unelected governments that oppose democracy and rule by fear. Democratically elected governments also need to support human rights and international law, if the vote of the people is to bring about justice and liberty.

TIANANMEN SQUARE
This memorial commemorates events in Beijing, the Chinese capital, in 1989. Students and workers gathered in Tiananmen Square to protest against government policies and corruption, and to ask for reform. The army was sent in and hundreds, some say thousands, of protesters were killed, injured, or arrested.

Inscription means "Democratic martyrs are immortal"

STAND UP FOR YOUR RIGHTS
This image of a lone protester standing in the path of a tank on Tiananmen Square in 1989 was seen around the world on television. As a result, the Chinese government came under enormous international pressure to address the concerns of the protesters. However, China did not bring in democratic reform and continued to ignore human rights.

THE FALL OF SADDAM
In 2003 the United States and United Kingdom invaded Iraq, which they claimed was developing "weapons of mass destruction." These were never found, but Iraq's brutal dictator, Saddam Hussein, was overthrown. Here, US troops pull down his statue. Democratic elections were held in 2005, but the country was still extremely unstable. The new government was weakened by fighting involving foreign troops, resistance fighters, rival militias, political factions, and terrorists.

OPPOSITION IN ZIMBABWE
With faces hidden to avoid recognition, supporters of the opposition Movement for Democratic Change (MDC) attend a rally in Zimbabwe in 2005. At a similar rally in 2007, MDC members were arrested and beaten up by police. The ruling Zimbabwean African National Union-Patriotic Front (ZANU-PF) party, led by Robert Mugabe, has been accused of attacking human rights, restricting political freedom, and rigging elections.

Flag of Zimbabwe

or burqa

Ballot paper

AFGHANISTAN ELECTION
A woman votes in Afghanistan in 2005. In 2001 US and British troops joined with a northern Afghan force to overthrow the country's Taliban government. Parliamentary elections followed. Under the Taliban, there had been no elections and conditions for women had been extremely restrictive.

The Basque flag

WHAT IS TERRORISM?
Terrorism is the use of violence to inspire fear in pursuit of political aims. Terror tactics such as those used by the Basque organization ETA, which seeks independence from Spain, include bombings and assassinations. Terrorism has been used by groups of many different political persuasions.

DISPUTE IN VENEZUELA
Opponents of Venezuelan President Hugo Chávez protest in 2007 against his refusal to renew the RCTV television station's license. The shutting down of the popular station was a blow for freedom of speech. However, Chávez's supporters claim that in 2002 RCTV backed an attempt to overthrow Chávez's democratically elected socialist government.

Marble memorial stands near the Chinese embassy, London

WHO MURDERED ANNA POLITKOVSKAYA?
This Russian journalist who campaigned for human rights was murdered in Moscow in 2006. She had written that Russian democracy was failing under President Vladimir Putin and had criticized Russia's war in Chechnya.

ARRESTED—FOR WINNING AN ELECTION
In 1988 Aung San Suu Kyi founded the National League for Democracy in Burma (Myanmar). Her party won a general election in 1990, but the country's military rulers refused to hand over power. Aung San Suu Kyi faced years of house arrest, imprisonment, and isolation from her family.

Democratic systems

"IT HAS BEEN SAID THAT DEMOCRACY IS the worst form of government, except for all the others that have been tried..." These were the words of English statesman Winston Churchill in 1947. But democratic government can take many forms, from constitutional monarchies to republics. Different systems of election may produce two large parties or many smaller ones. Perhaps the most important contrast is between presidential democracies, where the president is head of state and is chosen directly by the voters, and parliamentary democracies, where voters choose members of parliament, and the leader of one party, usually the largest, becomes prime minister.

CONSTITUTION DAY
Flags fly as Norwegians celebrate Constitution Day on May 17. A constitution is a set of laws that establishes how a nation rules itself. It may be voted on, challenged, and amended. Some countries, such as the United Kingdom, do not have a specially written constitution.

TWO CHAMBERS
Some parliaments are made up of a single assembly, known as a house or chamber. Others have two, a lower and an upper chamber. The upper chamber often reviews or revises the laws passed by the lower. Here, both of France's parliamentary chambers gather in 2005 for a special meeting to discuss changes to the French constitution. The meeting was at the former royal palace of Versailles.

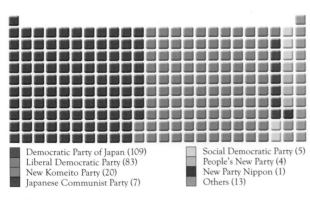

- Democratic Party of Japan (109)
- Liberal Democratic Party (83)
- New Komeito Party (20)
- Japanese Communist Party (7)
- Social Democratic Party (5)
- People's New Party (4)
- New Party Nippon (1)
- Others (13)

FORMING A GOVERNMENT
In Japan's House of Councilors election in 2007, the Democratic Party of Japan won the most seats, but it did not have a majority in the House. Where a party wins over 50 percent of the seats, it can form a government by itself and pass new laws. If no one party wins enough seats to have a clear majority, two or more parties may have to join together to form a government.

Binnenhof (Dutch parliament buildings) in The Hague

A PARLIAMENTARY SYSTEM
Like the UK, the Netherlands is a parliamentary democracy. Under this system, members of the winning party (or parties) in an election select a leader, known as the prime minister. In turn, the prime minister chooses a cabinet of ministers to decide policy and carry it out. The prime minister is head of government, but there may also be a head of state whose role is mainly ceremonial. In the Netherlands, a constitutional monarchy, the head of state is Queen Beatrix (left).

PRESIDENTIAL ELECTIONS

In the United States, each party selects its presidential candidate following "primary" elections held in individual states. The nation then votes in a presidential election. This badge was worn by supporters of Teddy Roosevelt in the 1904 election.

Theodore ("Teddy") Roosevelt gave his name to the first teddy bears

WHAT DOES A GOVERNMENT DO?

It is the job of an elected government to make laws. New legislation is put before parliament and voted on. Government ministers or secretaries also manage the economy, education, health and welfare, defense, and foreign relations. Here Russian president Vladimir Putin (left) meets Japanese prime minister Junichiro Koizumi (right) in 2005.

WHAT IS THE JUDICIARY?

Although the government makes the laws, it does not administer justice. That is the work of the judiciary (judges or magistrates), which is independent from the government. Judges are usually appointed, but in some countries they are elected. Judges often wear a formal costume in court.

Gavel, banged by American judges to bring the court to order

A PRESIDENT'S POWER

The United States is a republic organized as a presidential democracy. George W. Bush was elected to power twice, in 2000 and 2004. As chief executive, head of state, and commander-in-chief of the army, the president wields considerable power, but he may face a Congress in which the opposing party has a majority, as Bush did from 2006. This cannot happen in a parliamentary democracy.

ADMINISTRATION

Carrying out government business is the job of the civil service. In some countries, civil servants are appointed by the government on political lines. In others, they are expected to be independent of political parties. China's civil service is more than 2,000 years old. This official seal dates from the 1700s.

On a medieval war mace, this end would have been used to inflict injury; now it is purely ornamental

Entire mace is made of wood, covered in silver gilt

Shaft embellished with engravings

The power house

NATIONAL LEGISLATURES or parliaments are often housed in large buildings that include government and party offices, committee rooms, and the offices of elected representatives. The most important room is the chamber where representatives debate and vote on new legislation or government policy. The way in which legislation is prepared and put to the vote varies from one country to another. Procedures for voting must be fair, with an accurate count. Representatives generally vote for their own party, but may rebel if they disagree with a policy. Party officials (known in some countries as whips) try to keep the party united.

PEOPLE VERSUS GOVERNMENT
The clock tower of the British Houses of Parliament, with its famous bell (Big Ben), is a well-known London landmark. In February 2003 it was surrounded by the largest public protest in British history. Over a million people marched against the government's proposed invasion of Iraq. In a democracy, the government has to strike a politically acceptable balance between its own authority and popular opposition outside parliament.

WHERE LAWS ARE MADE
A national legislature is often (but not always) located in the capital city. It is known by different names in different countries, such as Parliament, Estates-General, Congress, Diet, Assembly, or Council. Some countries, such as the United States, Australia, and Germany, are federations of smaller states or territories. The federation has a national (federal) legislative assembly, but each state within the federation also has its own legislature. Some nonfederal nations devolve a degree of self-government to certain regions or territories, as the United Kingdom has done in Northern Ireland, Wales, and Scotland.

UNITED STATES
The United States federal legislature, called Congress, is sited in the city of Washington, DC. Congress is made up of a lower chamber, the House of Representatives, and an upper chamber, the Senate. Any new law must be passed by both houses.

CANADA
The Canadian Parliament is located in Ottawa, Ontario. It is made up of two chambers. The elected House of Commons holds the most power. The second chamber, the Senate, is appointed by the country's governor-general on behalf of the monarch.

NEW ZEALAND
New Zealand is a constitutional monarchy with a one-chamber parliament, the House of Representatives, sited in Wellington. The "Beehive" (above, left) houses the offices of the prime minister and cabinet, while debates take place in Parliament House (right).

Cross denotes the monarch as Defender of the Faith

SYMBOL OF AUTH RITY

No debate may begin in the United Kingdom's House of Commons until this ceremonial mace has been carried into the chamber. The UK is a constitutional monarchy, and the mace is an ancient symbol of royal authority. It reminds Members of Parliament (MPs) that the monarch has handed powers over to them, as representatives of the people. As head of state, the monarch still opens the new session of parliament each fall.

TEMPERS RUN HIGH

A brawl breaks out among members during a vote in the Taiwan parliament in 2007. Parliamentary debates are generally subject to strict rules and procedures. They are often chaired by an official known as the Speaker, whose job is to keep order. Some legislatures have seats arranged in an oval or circle. Others have seats in which the government and opposition face each other.

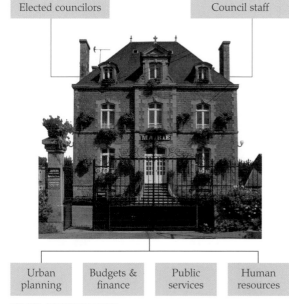

Elected councilors

Council staff

| Urban planning | Budgets & finance | Public services | Human resources |

LOCAL GOVERNMENT

This is a town hall in Normandy, France. There are often several tiers of democratic government below the national legislature. Councils may exist at the level of villages, towns, cities, counties, or departments. They generally include elected councilors and council staff, and may be headed by an elected mayor or similar official. Councils may deal with such local needs as planning, refuse collection, policing, or schools. They have limited powers of legislation and taxation.

GERMANY

This modern dome tops the 1894 Reichstag building in Berlin, home to the lower chamber of the German parliament. Germany is a federal republic. The president is the head of state, and the chancellor is the head of government. The lower chamber is called the Bundestag ("federal diet"). The upper chamber is called the Bundesrat ("federal council") and represents the German *Länder* (states).

HUNGARY

Hungary's parliament buildings overlook the Danube River, in the capital city of Budapest. Hungary is a republic and has a single-chamber National Assembly (the Országgyűlés) that also elects the head of state. The head of government is the prime minister.

JAPAN

Japan's national diet building is in Tokyo. It has two chambers, the House of Representatives and the House of Councilors. Japan is a constitutional monarchy. Its emperor is head of state and its prime minister is head of government.

Party politics

PLURALISM, THE MULTIPARTY SYSTEM of politics, is not the only model for democracy. In fact, it was strongly opposed by the first US president, George Washington. He claimed that political parties created divisions between people. Some election candidates run as independents, to avoid being connected to any party. However, most countries in the world have adopted a multiparty political system, and see it as an essential part of their democracy. Members of a party share similar political ideologies or ideas. Ordinary members of the party help to select candidates to run for election, raise funds, campaign for their party's candidates, and attend conferences where party policy is decided. Members do not agree about all policy questions, so they may need to make compromises for the sake of party unity. It is important that party leaders continue to listen to their members' views, so that parties are democratic.

Rosette in party color

PARTY LOYALTIES
A supporter of the Democratic Party for Macedonian Unity has painted her face in the red-and-yellow pattern of her national flag. She is attending a rally in Skopje, capital of the former Yugoslav Republic of Macedonia, during presidential elections in 2004. Parties can bring fierce loyalties and powerful opposition to the political process.

THE PARTY FAITHFUL
Democratic Party members from all over the United States celebrate at their National Convention in Boston in 2004. Rallies and conferences offer a chance for political parties to build up unity and morale, raise funds, and display their self-confidence to the public. Such events are often stage-managed for the television cameras. However, balloons and buttons may distract from the real business of politics—the development of serious ideas and practical policies by party members.

Tug-of-war based on the work of the political cartoonist Thomas Nast (1840–1902)

The donkey has been a symbol of the Democrats since 1837

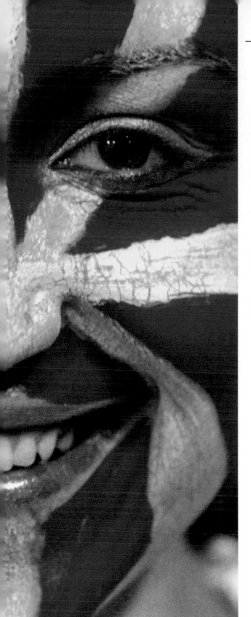

IT'S MY PARTY!
Political parties may promote their identity with logos, colors, banners, pop music, and even souvenir plates and mugs. Large parties spend vast sums on advertising and publicity. Smaller parties may find it hard to compete with the big players, who have the advantages of financial support, media interest, and powerful connections.

PARTY LEADER
Angela Merkel (right), leader of Germany's conservative Christian Democratic Union (CDU), faces the microphones. She became chancellor in 2005. Leaders play an important part in most parties. They must be able to communicate well with party members and with the public, both directly and through the media. Experience and good judgment are just as important in a leader as having a popular image.

TUG-OF-WAR
A cartoon shows the two largest parties in the United States, the Democrats and the Republicans, engaged in a struggle for power, represented by a tug-of-war. Is party politics too combative? Many parties play down political differences and look for the center ground, so they can appeal to most voters. Others believe that a contest between people of different views is what democracy is all about. After all, if all the parties are much the same, why bother to vote?

The elephant has represented Republicans since 1874

MONSTER RAVING LOONY
In the United Kingdom a joker and pop star called Screaming Lord Sutch (1940–1999) founded the Official Monster Raving Loony Party in 1983. He ran in more than 40 elections in order to mock pompous politicians. Was this a public service or a public waste of time?

Who represents you?

In THE DIRECT FORM OF DEMOCRACY, as in ancient Athens, each citizen votes on major issues of the day. However, that is just not practical when the electorate numbers many millions. Instead, people elect a representative or member of parliament to vote on their behalf. In each geographical area (often known as a constituency in a general election, or as a ward in a municipal election), people vote for someone to represent them. Elected members may be expected to represent the wider interests of the public, rather than just the views of those who voted for them. Political parties often try to choose election candidates from every part of society, including women and ethnic minorities.

EVERYDAY WORK
A representative needs an office in his or her constituency and another in the legislature, and a staff including secretaries, research assistants, and volunteers (known in the US as interns). Representatives bring local issues to the attention of government, talk to campaigners, and help individuals with any problems.

REPRESENTATIVES AND DELEGATES
Edmund Stoiber (left) and Erwin Huber are leading politicians from Germany's conservative Christian Social Union (CSU). Here they make their views known to the Bundesrat or federal council in 2004, as delegates from the state of Bavaria. A delegate is someone sent by another organization (such as a state or territorial assembly) to speak or vote on its behalf. In some assemblies, delegates may be mandated (instructed) to vote in particular way by the organization they represent.

Traditional dress of white djellaba (hooded cloak) is worn for the opening of parliament

MOROCCAN PARLIAMENT
Representatives wear traditional dress as they gather in Morocco's parliament. The lower chamber has 325 seats, of which 35 are now held by women. The Moroccan parliament has become more democratic since 1997, but the country's king still has strong personal powers. He can dissolve (shut down) parliament, for example, and appoint a new prime minister.

MAPS FOR DEMOCRACY
This map shows Canada's provinces and territories and its key indicates the number of seats or constituencies (known locally as ridings) in each one. The most populous regions have the largest numbers of representatives. Ontario, with its big cities, has 106 seats, while the sparsely populated Arctic wilderness of Nunavut has only one. It is important that the boundaries of constituencies can change if the population grows or declines, but also that they cannot be rigged to favor one party (see page 49).

KEY:

YT Yukon Territory – **1 seat**
NT Northwest Territories – **1 seat**
NU Nunavut – **1 seat**
BC British Columbia – **36 seats**
AB Alberta – **28 seats**
SK Saskatchewan – **14 seats**
MB Manitoba – **14 seats**
ON Ontario – **106 seats**

QC Québec – **75 seats**
NL Newfoundland & Labrador – **7 seats**
NB New Brunswick – **10 seats**
PE Prince Edward Island – **4 seats**
NS Novia Scotia – **11 seats**

IN THE COMMUNITY
French presidential candidate Ségolène Royal visits a textile factory in Brittany during her failed campaign of 2007. Democratic politicians need to keep in touch with ordinary people, and not only talk to them but also listen to their concerns.

CHINESE NATIONAL PEOPLE'S CONGRESS
The Chinese legislature has several tiers. People vote directly for local representatives. Delegates from local assemblies make up the regional and national congresses, which are dominated by members of the Chinese Communist Party (CCP). The CCP also runs the national congress's everyday business.

How elections work

THE VOTE IS THE KEY to any democratic system of government, as this is how the people have their say. Sometimes voters may be asked to decide a question directly by voting in a referendum (which means "thing to be referred") or a plebiscite (a "people's resolution"). This form of democracy is used to change the constitution or resolve a major policy issue. More often, people vote in local constituencies to choose their representatives, or to elect a president. In these elections different systems of voting may be used. The simplest is one where the candidate with the most votes is declared the winner. However, this may mean that small parties win very few seats, so a form of proportional representation is often thought to be fairer—in this system, parties are allocated seats according to the percentage of the vote that they win nationwide.

BALLOT PAPER
A vote may be recorded with a simple "X" next to the chosen candidate (or with a number, if the candidates are to be ranked in order of preference). For a fair election, the ballot paper must be designed so that the instructions to voters are absolutely clear.

FIRST-PAST-THE-POST
In this British cartoon of 1867, the political system is shown as a horse race, being won by the Conservative leader Benjamin Disraeli. The type of election in which the candidate with the most votes wins is sometimes called first-past-the-post (as when a horse crosses the finishing line). It has also been called winner-takes-all or simple majority.

ELECTION TACTICS
Zulus supporting the Inkatha Freedom Party (IFP) demonstrate in traditional dress during South African elections. In 2004 the IFP gave up a ten-year power-sharing deal with the ruling African National Congress (ANC) and joined a coalition of opposition parties. Before, during, or after elections, political parties may form alliances or decide to share power with other parties. However, such political wheeling and dealing can mean compromising on ideals and can confuse or even anger supporters.

THE NUMBERS GAME
A winning candidate speaks at an election in Birmingham, England. The first-past-the-post system is straightforward and votes can be easily counted. However, the winner may have been chosen by only 30 percent of the electorate—so the preferences of the other 70 percent are ignored. In some countries, voters rank candidates in numerical order, and votes are transferred from less to more popular candidates until an overall winner emerges.

JOINING IN

"Join in!" says the slogan on the campaign bus of Germany's Green Party. The Greens formed part of national coalition governments in Germany from 1998 to 2005. Coalition governments represent a wider share of opinion, but are sometimes criticized as less effective because they have to water down their ideas. Electoral systems based on proportional representation give more of a chance to smaller political parties and this tends to result in more coalition governments.

PUBLIC PROPOSITIONS

The governor of the state of California, former movie star Arnold Schwarzenegger, debates a series of legislative proposals, known as initiatives or propositions. These can be put forward for a state ballot by any members of the public or campaigning groups who can gather enough supporters. Similar direct ballots are held in other countries. In Italy, a referendum can be held if 500,000 or more people petition for a piece of legislation to be overturned.

ELECTING THE ELECTORS

US presidential candidates take part in a TV debate. Although the whole American public votes in the presidential election, their votes do not directly decide who will become president. The election result in each state determines which voters will go on to make up the "electoral college"—the 538 people whose votes will actually decide who becomes the president.

SWISS REFERENDUM

Referendums are a way of life in Switzerland, where they are held three or four times a year at all levels of government. Referendums are said to make politicians think twice before bringing in any hasty legislation. However, critics of frequent referendums believe that the mandate given to the winner at a general election entitles the government to get on with its job without too much interference.

Polling day

VOTE HERE
A polling station must be secure, with impartial staff. It must also be clearly signposted and any instructions easily understood. The sign on this California station reflects the first languages of local citizens—English, Chinese, Korean, Japanese, Spanish, Tagalog (a language of the Philippines), and Vietnamese.

THE BALLOT BOX
A Nenets woman casts her vote at a mobile polling station in the Russian Arctic. Ballot boxes must be sturdy and padlocked. They must be transported securely to the count. In fraudulent elections, ballot boxes are often "lost" or tampered with.

THE PERIOD BEFORE AN ELECTION is an extremely busy time. Each party sets out its platform (plans for policy), campaigns around the country, and conducts media interviews. Finally the big moment arrives. In some countries, such as Australia, voting is compulsory. Polling may take place on a single day or over a longer period. It usually takes place in public buildings, such as schools. Polling stations must be easy to get to, and open at convenient times. To avoid fraud, voters must often register beforehand and have their identity checked on the day. A booth is generally set up so that the ballot paper can be filled out in private. International observers may be called in to check whether an election has been carried out fairly and freely.

OVERSEAS VOTERS
Citizens living abroad can usually vote in their own national elections. They may vote by mail or go in person to vote at their country's embassy. These papers and passport were used by an Iraqi citizen to register for her vote in Iraq's 2005 election, at a polling station in Munich, Germany.

Nenets woman places her voting slip into padlocked ballot box

VOTING BY MAIL

Postal voting allows people to send in their ballot papers by mail. This mailbox is in the Republic of Ireland, where postal votes may be made by students living away from home, or by people who cannot reach a polling station because of illness or disability. Increasingly, postal ballots are being offered to all voters, but critics worry about security and lack of secrecy.

ELECTRONIC VOTING

A woman tries out an electronic voting machine in a mock election in Bhutan in 2007. This tiny Himalayan nation, long an absolute monarchy, was preparing for the introduction of multiparty democracy. Computer voting is simple, quick, and cheap, but critics fear that it, too, may be open to fraud.

THE BIG COUNT

The polls have closed and the ballot boxes have been brought to the count during a British election. The votes are counted by hand. Any ballot papers that have been spoiled (defaced or filled in incorrectly) are discounted. If the result for two candidates is very close, there may be a recount, to check that there have been no errors.

GOLD FINGER

This stylish pointing stick was used until the 18th century to count votes in the Italian republic of Venice (see page 13). The new doge or leader was elected by committee, in a fiendishly complicated process.

KEEPING TALLY

Election officials in Bakau, in the West African state of Gambia, keep a tally of the election count by placing marbles on a board, during the 2006 presidential elections.

*Index finger
in gold*

*Thumb presses
firmly on keypad*

*Undetached or hanging
chad (square of paper
from punch-card ballot)*

PUNCH-CARD BALLOTS

Another way to register a ballot is by using a machine to punch a hole into the card. This should be simple enough, but it caused confusion in Florida during the US presidential election of 2000. The problem was that some holes had been pressed but not punctured (dimpled chads) while others had been only partially punctured (hanging chads). Should these be counted as valid votes?

Held to account

ONCE GOVERNMENTS HAVE BEEN ELECTED, they have the right to take executive action. At the same time, they must never forget that they remain the servants of the people. Democracy does not end with the ballot box. Governments have a duty to be honest, to obey domestic and international law, to uphold human rights, and to work for the public good rather than personal gain. They should be transparent, not secretive, in their actions. Democratic constitutions often contain a series of checks and balances, to ensure that no head of state gains too much power and that representatives may be held to account for their actions. Committees, public inquiries, or independent officials may investigate any accusations of wrongdoing.

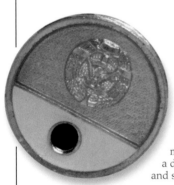

Stasi lapel badge

STATE SECRETS REVEALED
The German Democratic Republic, which ruled East Germany from 1949 to 1990, used informers and secret agents to spy on its own citizens. Some 33 million pages of files were found in the archives of its ministry for state security, or Stasi (right). In a democracy, the government's power to gather and store secret data should be strictly limited.

THE BALANCE OF POWER
Riot police clash with demonstrators in Taiwan. Governments have a duty to maintain law and order and defend the state. However, they also have a duty to allow freedom of speech and political protest. Repressive governments may use the police or armed forces to silence anyone who opposes their policies. Some governments even resort to the torture and illegal detention (imprisonment) of opponents.

IT'S A GERRYMANDER!

In 1812, Massachusetts governor Elbridge Gerry approved new, convoluted electoral borders that favored the Democrats. A cartoonist of the day showed how the electoral map now resembled a salamander. He coined the word "gerrymander," meaning to redraw constituency boundaries so as to include more supporters and deliver more votes to one party.

Town's borders redrawn

BRIBERY AND CORRUPTION

This American money box shows William M. Tweed, a notoriously corrupt New York politician of the 1860s. Tweed was jailed for stealing millions of dollars from the city. Government corruption, such as taking bribes, embezzling (stealing) public money, or rigging elections, is still a problem today.

Money box shaped like William "the Boss" Tweed

Richard Nixon

USA 32

REMOVAL FROM POWER

Many constitutions allow charges to be brought against an offending president or government official. This process, called impeachment, may lead to a criminal trial. US President Richard Nixon (left) resigned in 1974 before impeachment hearings against him went ahead. He had been accused of attempting to cover up a burglary of the Democratic headquarters in Washington's Watergate complex.

CAMPAIGNING FOR JUSTICE

Women in Santiago, Chile, light candles in memory of loved ones who "disappeared" during the murderous rule of General Pinochet. The event was organized in 2001 by Amnesty International, an organization that campaigns for the release of political prisoners. Groups such as Amnesty have been very successful at holding governments to account.

Taking part

THE STRUGGLE TO ACHIEVE DEMOCRACY goes on. In many countries the number of people turning out to vote in elections has fallen in recent years. Democracy only thrives if citizens are active. Policies need to be debated—whether informally among friends, or at public meetings, or through the media. Then people are informed enough to vote on policies at the next election. Those who approve of how society is organized need to campaign to keep it that way. Those who do not should do their best to change it. They may join an existing political party, or form a new one with people who share similar ideas.

A CLASSROOM VOTE
Could this be a future US president? Pupils in Denver, Colorado, hold a mock election at their school. A successful democracy needs to teach its citizens how the system works, and encourage everyone to take part.

OPINION POLL
An Australian takes part in an opinion poll. Should the country remain a monarchy or become a republic? Polls only find out the views of a small percentage of the electorate. However, they help to measure public opinion between elections and serve as a useful guide for politicians, campaigners, and the wider public.

Each banner reads "Save the climate, now"

FINDING A VOICE
How can individuals get across their point of view to governments? They can meet with their elected representatives or write letters. They can also join campaign groups, some of which lobby or persuade governments around the world. The Worldwide Fund for Nature (WWF) campaigns for conservation, Greenpeace for the environment, and Amnesty for human rights.

CIVIL SOCIETY
Greenpeace members gather on Mount Ararat, Turkey, in May 2007, holding banners to alert the world to the dangers of global warming. Campaigning movements such as Greenpeace belong to what is sometimes called civil society. This sector of society is made up of all kinds of voluntary organizations that are run by active citizens. They include professional bodies, trade unions, religious groups, educational or cultural associations, women's groups, and charities. This civil sector works in partnership with the social sector (made up of state-backed institutions) and the commercial sector (made up of businesses) to create a dynamic democracy.

PUBLIC MEETING
Ever since the days of democracy in ancient Athens, public speaking has been an important part of the political process. People are able to argue for and against different courses of action, and persuade others to come around to their point of view.

COMMON GROUND
Hispanic Americans campaign for immigrant rights at a rally in Chicago. Activists with a common ethnic background often join together as a pressure group. Within a party they may form a "caucus," to put forward their ideas or support a particular candidate. Other common-interest groups include professional associations, trade unions, faith groups, and youth sections.

Model ark built on Mount Ararat, where Noah's Ark was said to have come to rest after the Great Flood

Ark raises awareness of floods and other dangers associated with global warming

FOUNDING A NEW PARTY
The Russian Garry Kasparov speaks to the press at a protest in St. Petersburg. Once one of the world's leading chess players, Kasparov retired from the game in 2005 in order to campaign for democracy and form a coalition against President Vladimir Putin. Founding a new party is difficult in any country where one or two big parties dominate the political scene. Activists need to draw up a party constitution, raise funds, recruit members, and draw up policies. They may need to be brave as well, if they face intimidation or violence from established parties.

Protest!

Voters hope to elect a government that they can support. However, if their favored candidate does not win, they still have to accept the result of the election, provided it was fair. They will get a chance to vote for their candidate again at the next election. In the meantime, they can campaign for change on any issues that are especially important to them. In a democracy, opposition groups should have a legal right to voice their disapproval of the government. Sometimes protesters go further and break the law, just as the suffragettes did in order to win votes for women. This is called civil disobedience. Many people feel that civil disobedience is acceptable, as long as protesters are not violent and take full responsibility for their actions. If citizens believe that their government is behaving illegally, protest may not be enough. Instead, they may be able to take the government to court.

Megaphone

WORD OF MOUTH
What are the limits of free speech? They vary greatly and are constantly challenged. Many democratic governments allow public criticism, but pass laws to forbid language that is racist, offensive, or likely to cause violence or public disorder.

LEGAL CHALLENGE
Pakistani democrats, opposed to General Pervez Musharraf's government, protest in Karachi in 2007 against the suspension of Chief Justice Iftikhar Muhammad Chaudhry. In a democracy, an independent system of justice provides people with a legal channel through which to challenge government action.

GLOBAL POWER
German riot police face down protesters opposed to global capitalism. The occasion is the 2007 summit meeting of leaders from the world's most powerful and rich nations, the G8 (or "Group of Eight"). In a global economy, international institutions can take actions that affect the daily lives of millions of people. Voting for a change of national government may not be enough to influence these international policies. Public protest may be the only option.

VIOLENT PROTEST

A car is set ablaze by angry youths in a suburb of Paris during riots in 2005. Protest that endangers life and public safety cannot be acceptable. Governments have a duty to protect their citizens. In order to prevent such attacks, governments need to enforce the law, but also investigate reasons for violence. It may result from social injustice, poverty, or a failure of the democratic process.

PEACEFUL PROTEST

Antiwar demonstrator Brian Haw set up camp outside the British Houses of Parliament in 2001, protesting silently. Laws were passed to limit the right to protest near Parliament, and Haw's posters and possessions were removed by police, but his protest continued. Here he is joined by other demonstrators, who cover their faces with his photograph.

CHAMPION OF FREE SPEECH

Turkish author Orhan Pamuk won the Nobel Prize for Literature in 2006. However, his discussions about Turkish history and the massacre of Armenians in 1915 led to bitter criticism of him in Turkey. He was taken to court and accused of insulting his homeland. Charges against him were eventually dropped.

ON STRIKE

Taxi drivers in Beijing, China, strike for a day in 2000 to protest about rising fuel prices. A strike is another form of protest sometimes used against governments. In a general strike, all workers withhold their labor.

ROCKING FOR THE FARMERS

Popular musicians sometimes use their fame to support campaigns of public protest. Here, Canadian rock star Neil Young launches US Farm Aid 2006. This series of yearly concerts draws attention to the problems faced by small-scale farmers in the United States.

The fourth estate

MAKING FUN
Just as jesters were allowed to mock medieval kings, the media in a healthy democracy can make fun of candidates or elected politicians through cartoons and comedy shows.

IN MEDIEVAL EUROPE, politics was primarily conducted by three "estates" or classes—the nobility, the clergy, and the commons. Since the 1800s there has also been, according to some writers, a "fourth estate"— the press. At first this only meant newspapers, but now it has expanded to include the whole range of modern communications media, such as radio, television, and Internet. Some media work in the public interest and serve democracy. Others represent the interests of their owners. The media provide a channel for valuable information, but they may also be used by politicians to manipulate or influence public opinion.

TELLING IT LIKE IT IS
Wearing a protective flak jacket, a reporter covers the 2006 Israel–Lebanon War. The information that people receive through news reports on television, the Internet, or in the printed press enables them to make their own political judgments, rather than relying on government information. That is why it is vital to democracy that news is reported as factually and as fairly as possible.

THE IMPACT OF TELEVISION
The Qatar-based Aljazeera television news channel uses satellite and Internet broadcasts to reach a new Middle Eastern audience, previously accustomed only to state-controlled broadcasting, as well as other viewers around the world. Television has transformed the nature of international politics.

"You should not spread antisocial materials on the Internet"

这些反社会的言论，不能在网吧传播……

3、互联网上网服务营业场所经营单位和上网消费者不得利用互联网上网服务营业场所制作、下载、复制、查阅、发布、传播或者以其他方式使用含有下列内容的信息：
（一）反对宪法确定的基本原则的；

根据举报，你在网吧上网发布危害国家统一的言论，跟我们走一趟！

（二）危害国家统一、主权和领土完整的；

"Come with me, please. You have published materials to harm the unity of the nation"

WEB WARNING
A Chinese poster warns users of an Internet café to obey government guidelines. The Internet is generally beyond the control of national governments, although there is some censorship. On the Internet, people are free to express their ideas and criticize oppressive governments. Once such opinions have been posted, they may be read by people all over the world.

STUDIO LIGHTS
Nancy Pelosi, a leading Democrat and Speaker of the US House of Representatives, appears on *The Tonight Show* with Jay Leno in 2007. The image that politicians present on television can often make or break their career—and decide the fortune of their parties in an election.

L'Unità, which Berlusconi claimed was politically biased against him

ON THE NEWSSTAND

Newspapers encourage democracy by providing the public with news, information, commentary, opinion, and investigations. They may alert politicians to social problems or hold them to account—make them answerable for their actions. Readers must remember that newspapers, too, often have a political agenda of their own, and this may show in the way certain news stories are selected or edited. That is why it is important to have access to a variety of news. Another problem is that some popular newspapers oversimplify issues that are complicated.

The German newspaper Die Welt (The World) sells in more than 130 countries

MEDIA POWER

Silvio Berlusconi brandishes an opposition party newspaper while campaigning in 2006. Berlusconi, the richest man in Italy, was twice elected prime minister while he owned major newspapers and three television channels that broadcast his views. Powerful media owners are sometimes called "press barons."

The American International Herald Tribune is delivered to more than 180 countries each day

GAGGED!

A poster draws attention to the problem of extreme censorship. In many countries, journalists risk jail or death when they investigate corruption or write articles that criticize the government. A free and independent press is essential for a democracy to function properly.

Stateless and voteless

IN ANCIENT ATHENS, non-Athenian residents were excluded from the vote. In ancient Rome, political debate raged about who should be counted as citizens of the empire. Questions of citizenship, nationality, and residency are still part of public argument about the franchise today. They become more pressing as large numbers of refugees flee wars, racial or religious persecution, natural disasters, or grinding poverty. Many end up living in refugee camps. Others seek asylum (safety) abroad. Migrants may find legal work, but suffer discrimination and receive low wages. If their new country restricts immigration, they may be forced to work illegally. Without the support of a state, migrants have few rights and no voice. They cannot vote, and so they have no representation.

CITIZENSHIP
Passports and papers are needed to travel or settle in another country. Without them, a migrant cannot find legal work or register for public assistance. In order to secure a full set of rights, including the right to vote in national elections, immigrants must apply to become legal citizens.

WHEN SOCIETY BREAKS DOWN…
Former refugees from the Hutu ethnic group leave a retraining camp in Rwanda in 1997. Three years earlier, Hutus had massacred more than 800,000 people, mostly Tutsis. The terrible violence spilled into neighboring countries and created hundreds of thousands of refugees.

PEOPLE ADRIFT
A Spanish patrol vessel looking for would-be migrants came across this Senegalese fishing boat off West Africa in 2007. Economic migrants are often exploited by criminals called human traffickers, who charge them large sums of money to be packed into boats or trucks and smuggled into another country.

IN DETENTION
Asylum seekers break out of a detention center in Woomera, Australia, in 2002. They were encouraged by sympathetic Australians who were protesting about their government's policy of detaining all asylum seekers, including children.

ILLEGAL IMMIGRANTS

A US patrol car checks the Mexican border for illegal migrants. Many poor Mexicans have crossed the border in search of a better life in the United States. Around 12 million people now live in the United States without official papers, of whom 57 percent are Mexican. These people remain unrepresented in the political system.

NEW CITIZENS

Two women, one Vietnamese and one Ghanaian, take an oath of allegiance as they become legal citizens of the United States at a special ceremony. This process is called naturalization. It gives immigrants full legal rights including the right to vote in elections.

PLIGHT OF THE REFUGEE

A Red Cross worker carries the baby of a would-be immigrant, intercepted at the port of Motril, Spain. Economic refugees face being returned to poverty. Political refugees face being returned to persecution, jail, or even death. Their rights are protected by an international treaty, the 1951 Geneva Convention for Refugees.

WORKERS FROM ABROAD

Migrant laborers from Eastern Europe plant cabbages at a farm in England. They work hard for low wages. Democratic governments have a duty to care for all the people living in a country, not just their own citizens. If resources such as jobs or healthcare are limited, governments may restrict immigration.

The big picture

As long as nations have existed, they have made alliances with other countries. In the last hundred years this process has gone further, with the creation of large treaty organizations, where a group of governments have agreed to work together. Global examples include the League of Nations (1919–1946) and the United Nations (UN, founded 1945). Governments send delegates to vote on their behalf at meetings of these global assemblies. These delegates are usually chosen by the government, not elected as representatives by the people. One exception is the European Union (EU), a political and economic alliance that has set up its own parliament with legislative powers—an experiment in democracy on an international scale. People in the EU vote for their members of the EU Parliament.

UNITED NATIONS
The UN has 192 member states, whose delegates vote at a General Assembly. The organization is headed by a General Secretary and has a powerful 15-member Security Council and an International Court of Justice. Its many agencies include the World Health Organization.

Knotted barrel is a symbol of peace

Gun is loaded but cannot fire

Non-Violence (1980), a sculpture by Karl Fredrik Reutersward

INTERNATIONAL ACTION
An observer from the UN looks on as ballot papers are counted in the tiny nation of Timor-Leste, which broke away from Indonesia in 2002 amid widespread violence. In fledgling democracies, it helps for people to know that outsiders are checking that their elections are fair. International organizations have played a major part in the spread of representative multiparty democracy.

THE AFRICAN UNION
Formed in 2001, the African Union (AU) is establishing a Pan-African Parliament, with 265 delegates from 53 member states. The AU aims to promote democracy, improve the economy, and resolve conflict. International treaty organizations like the AU may be based on military alliances, economic markets, common ownership of resources, former colonial ties, or geographical regions.

SWEDISH FOR "YES"
"Yes" buttons are prepared in 2003 for a Swedish referendum on whether or not to adopt the Euro as currency. In the end, 56 percent of Swedes voted against the proposal. Fifteen EU states have adopted the currency, and together make up the so-called Eurozone. With its alliance of different governments and interests, the EU's politics rarely run smoothly—but they do run peacefully.

PEOPLE TO PEOPLE
Latvian choristers perform in a competition at Bremen in Germany. While politicians make alliances between governments, bridge-building can also take place on a more personal level, through music festivals, sporting events, school exchanges, and holidays.

THE EUROPEAN UNION
The EU's founders hoped to end centuries of conflict between European nations. Today the union has 27 member states. Each must be a democracy with a record of respecting human rights. Another requirement is having a market economy—an economy where prices are set by buyers and sellers, rather than fixed by government.

Cylinder is a replica of a .45-caliber revolver's

SHARING PROBLEMS
Scientists monitor glaciers like this one in Alaska to keep track of climate change. Some of today's problems are on a global scale and can only be tackled by international action. It is important that ordinary people understand the issues and are able to have their say in crucial political decisions. They may not have direct access to international organizations, but they can put pressure on their own government to represent their views.

VOTE FOR PEACE
This sculpture stands in the grounds of the UN headquarters, built on international territory within New York City. The giant knotted revolver, a symbol of peace, was presented to the UN in 1988 by the small nation of Luxembourg. It reminds delegates that, as Winston Churchill said in 1954, "to jaw-jaw [talk] is better than to war-war."

The voting habit

VOTING IS NOT JUST USED IN POLITICS and government. As a form of group decision-making, it plays a major part in our daily lives. Its use varies from the serious to the entertaining. Voting takes place in businesses, in the workplace, in religious organizations, in schools, in the arts, and in sports. Usually only a small number of voters are involved. However, television game shows may inspire millions of viewers to cast a vote—in some cases, the turnout is higher than for a political election. Mass voting by the public has been made easier by modern communications technology, with votes being registered by cell phone or the Internet.

SALES BOYCOTT

A bumper sticker on a Saudi Arabian car urges people not to buy Danish goods, following a Danish newspaper's publication of cartoons thought to be offensive to Muslims. Refusing to buy goods for political, religious, or other reasons is called "voting with your wallet." It is a choice by the consumer and can be an effective form of protest.

Danish flag is crossed out, to symbolize the boycott of Danish goods

Lockable drawer for each academy member's vote

WORKERS' BALLOT

The count goes on as German telecom workers vote to strike in a trade union ballot. At issue is a company's decision to outsource or put out 50,000 jobs to another firm, whose workers receive lower wages for longer hours. The outcomes of strike votes often have great economic, political, and legal importance, so trade unions must carefully follow democratic procedures.

COMPANY BUSINESS

Shareholders assemble for the 2004 meeting of the Walt Disney Company. Forty-three percent refused to vote for the reelection of Michael Eisner as company chairman. He was replaced in that role by George J. Mitchell. Voting by shareholders plays a crucial role in the world of business. It can determine the staff a company may employ and the new directions a company may take.

Television screen shows white smoke billowing from the chimney of Sistine Chapel in the Vatican, Rome

BLACK SMOKE, WHITE SMOKE
The Pope, the head of the Roman Catholic Church, is elected by 120 cardinals. After each of the early ballots the papers are burned, giving off black smoke. When the new Pope is finally chosen, ballot papers are burned with a chemical to produce white smoke, a sign to the waiting crowds outside.

Golden Oscar statuette

AND THE WINNER IS...
The most famous awards for the film industry are the Oscars, presented since 1929 by the Academy of Motion Picture Arts and Sciences in Los Angeles, CA. The awards are voted for by 5,830 members and handed to the stars during a glittering ceremony.

THE ARTISTS' CHOICE
This elegant box was used to hold the ballots of Spain's leading artists, as they voted on whether or not to elect new members to the San Fernando Royal Academy of Fine Arts. The academy was founded in Madrid in 1744. Its most famous director was Francisco Goya.

OLYMPIC VOTES
The choice of city to host the Olympic Games every four years is hotly contested. It is voted on by the International Olympic Committee. The winner for 2008 was Beijing, China and the choice for 2012 was London, England.

Newly appointed university chancellor Chris Patten

THE DONS' DEBATE
Dons (academics) and former students at Oxford University, England, elected Chris Patten, the former Governor of Hong Kong, as their chancellor in 2003. There was little campaigning and the job paid no wages—yet the election was followed with great interest.

POP IDOL
The *Pop Idol* talent contest for new pop singers was first broadcast on British television in 2001 and now has spinoffs on every continent. Viewers vote for their favorite performer on the show's website, or by texting, phoning, or pressing the TV's digital interactive button.

Tomorrow's voters

Since the birth of democracy in the classical age, the world has undergone many social, economic, and political changes. The future will pose even greater challenges. How many more people can live on the planet? Are there enough resources to support them? Will climate change make large areas of Earth uninhabitable? Political systems will certainly have to adapt and develop in this changing world. Might nation-states be replaced by world government? How can people best control the way in which they are governed? It is not just a question of new technology for voting, or fairer methods of representation, although these are important. It is also a question of how citizens can use their vote to create a world based on liberty, peace, and justice.

Doctor

Newborn baby—one of nearly 300 born in the world every minute

WHAT NEXT FOR KOWLOON?
With around 111,500 people per square mile (43,000 per square km), the crowded Kowloon district of Hong Kong gives a glimpse into the possible future if world population growth continues. As a region of China, Hong Kong is governed by an elected legislative council that has limited powers. What will the future hold?

FUTURE CITIZENS
In 1900 the world population was about 1.6 billion. Today the figure is about 6.6 billion. World population may pass the 9 billion mark in around 2042. Population growth is highest in poorer, less developed countries. Voting systems and representative democracies will have to cope with this rapid rise in population. Planners will have to deal with the problems of poverty and provide enough education.

Apartment block is home to hundreds of families

CHILDREN OF HOPE

Child "peace messengers" from Yokohama, Japan, discuss the future with a UN representative in New York in 2005. They updated the UN on their peace work and gave money to the United Nations Children's Fund (UNICEF). Children around the world are interested in international issues, but not all are able to make their voices heard.

WATER FOR LIFE

This Ghanaian boy has just collected water from a pump provided by an international charity called WaterAid. Modern governments face great challenges to overcome inequality, poverty, and environmental problems. If they are to fulfill the ideals of democracy, they must work toward providing a future for all children.

SECURITY OR LIBERTY?

Closed-circuit television (CCTV) cameras are monitored by a private company at a secret underground bunker in London. The UK has more surveillance cameras per person than any other country in the world, perhaps one for every 14 citizens. In a democratic state, is this a welcome tool in the fight against crime, or part of a state intelligence network that could be used to attack civil liberties?

VOTING IN SPACE

In 2004 astronaut Leroy Chiao voted in the US presidential elections from the International Space Station (ISS), more than 225 miles (360 km) above Earth. He used his computer keyboard to cast a secret vote. Voting technology must adapt to ever-changing circumstances, including the need to vote in space.

World facts and figures

WHAT IS THE STATE of democracy in the 21st century? Large numbers of the world's citizens still live without the right to vote freely. Fortunately, rule by the military or dictators is becoming rarer. Where it does happen, it is often opposed by brave citizens. Voting rights—and civil rights in general—have been greatly extended in the last century. However, even democratic countries make alliances with oppressive regimes, or sometimes refuse to recognize democratically elected governments. The long campaign for democracy goes on.

CHANGING FACE OF SOUTH AMERICA
In 2006 Michelle Bachelet was elected Chile's first woman president—a hopeful sign of her country's move toward greater democracy. Bachelet's own father was tortured in prison when General Augusto Pinochet was dictator of Chile (1973–1990). The South American continent has a history of dictatorship and military rule.

Electorate size (millions)

0 50 100 150 200 250 300 350 400 450 500 550 600

India's total population is expected to reach 1.6 billion by 2050

India, USA, Indonesia, Russia, Japan, Brazil, Bangladesh, Germany, Mexico, Pakistan, Nigeria, Italy, UK, France, Philippines

Brazil has the largest number of voters in South America

Mexico has the largest number of Spanish-speaking voters

PEOPLE AND POWER
This chart shows the number of registered voters in the world's 15 largest democracies. The size of the electorate in India, where the population forms 17 percent of the world's total, dwarfs that of other democracies. Of course, political power comes from wealth, not size. The United States is the world's most powerful nation, but accounts for only 5 percent of the world's total population.

THE NUMBERS GAME
Numbers determine who wins an election—but the results are often far from straightforward. That is why countries sometimes revise their electoral rules. Haiti did just that after its 2006 election (right), only the fourth in the country's history, ended in disputes and violence. René Préval of the Lespwa coalition was voted president, but it was unclear whether he had won 48.8 percent of the 2.2 million votes, or 51.1 percent.

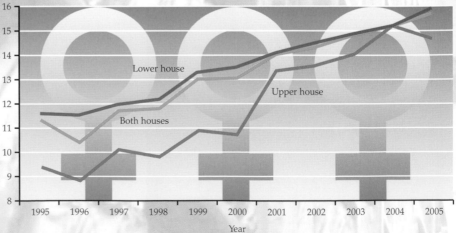

TYPES OF GOVERNMENT
Eighty-five percent of nations now stage multiparty elections, either as republics or as constitutional monarchies. This marks considerable progress. However, some of these nations still have limited suffrage and in some, the political system favors one economic, social, or ethnic group. Twelve percent of nations remain under authoritarian or single-party rule, absolute monarchy, or dictatorship. Three percent are disputed or in the process of change.

VOTING FOR WOMEN REPRESENTATIVES
Women make up half the world's population, but in the year 2005 there was not one parliament where female representatives occupied half the seats. Rwanda had 49 percent, the United Kingdom 20 percent, and the United States 15 percent. The global averages shown here range from 8 to 16 percent, but within this low band, the number is increasing steadily.

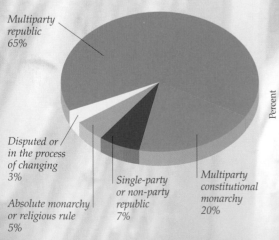

Multiparty republic 65%

Disputed or in the process of changing 3%

Absolute monarchy or religious rule 5%

Single-party or non-party republic 7%

Multiparty constitutional monarchy 20%

Lower house

Upper house

Both houses

Percent

16 15 14 13 12 11 10 9 8

1995 1996 1997 1998 1999 2000 2001 2002 2003 2004 2005

Year

THE DEVELOPMENT FACTOR

This map shows the world graded according to the UN Human Development Index. The index measures the well-being of nations in terms of health, education, and standard of living. At first glance these factors may not seem to be connected to voting, but they are all key in the development of stable, working democracies. The alternatives—disease, ignorance, and poverty—are serious obstacles. In fact, the common people's lack of education was one of the strongest arguments put forward by ancient Greek opponents of democracy.

KEY

- High development
- Medium development
- Low development
- Not ranked

Proportional representation system 38%

Partial proportional representation system 12%

Simple majority system 13.6%

Variety of voting systems 36.4%

VOTING SYSTEMS

There are more voting systems in use today than ever before. Fifty percent of countries use various proportional representation (PR) systems or part-PR systems. Only 13.6 percent of countries still use the first-past-the-post or simple majority system and nothing else. Other countries use different systems for different elections. In the United Kingdom, for example, the general election is first-past-the-post, but PR and other systems are used for European, Scottish, Welsh, and Northern Irish elections.

VOTER TURNOUT

This chart shows what percentage of the electorate has turned out to vote in five selected nations, including Italy, which has the highest turnout, and Mali, which has the lowest. Mali has only had elections since the 1990s, and its turnout is steadily rising. The general trend, however, is that turnout is falling in many of the more established democracies. Is the electorate becoming lazy and taking democracy for granted? Or are the politicians failing to connect with the public? Both citizens and representatives need to work for active democracy.

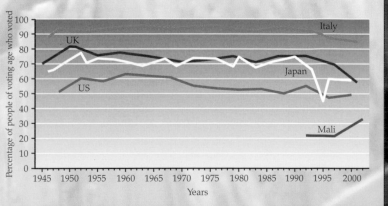

Timeline of democracy

THIS SELECTION OF HISTORICAL EVENTS traces the dramatic story of voting, and of assemblies, parliaments, and other legislatures around the world. It shows some of the advances and setbacks on the road to democracy, and some of the revolutions that changed not only history, but also how we think about people power today. Just what a democracy should be has always been argued over—and probably always will be.

An Athenian *ostrakon* (or vote for exile) from 400s BCE

BCE (Before Common Era)

c. 2650 ASSEMBLIES IN SUMER
Rulers of city-states in Sumer (southern Iraq) govern with the consent of citizens' assemblies.

c. 1000–c. 500 ASSEMBLIES IN INDIA
Evidence of citizens' assemblies and republics in parts of ancient India.

594 SOLON PAVES THE WAY
The statesman Solon reduces the powers of the ruling class in the Greek city-state of Athens, laying the foundations for democracy.

509 ROMAN REPUBLIC
Rome overthrows the monarchy.

508 PEOPLE POWER IN ATHENS
Kleisthenes introduces reforms known as *isonomía* ("equality of political rights"), or later as *demokratía* ("rule by the people").

461 DEATH OF AN ATHENIAN DEMOCRAT
The reformer Ephialtes is assassinated.

461–429 THE AGE OF PERIKLES
Athenian democracy flourishes under the leadership of Perikles.

366 PEOPLE'S CONSULS IN ROME
Roman leaders (consuls) may now be chosen from the common people (plebeians).

27 ROME BECOMES AN EMPIRE
The Roman Senate grants the title "Augustus" to Octavian, and Rome effectively ceases to be a republic.

CE (Common Era)

476 AGE OF KINGS
Fall of the Roman empire in the west. Most of Europe is ruled by small monarchies until the rise of Charlemagne's empire in the 800s.

600S–1066 COUNCILS OF THE WISE
Anglo-Saxon witenagemots (assemblies of wise councilors) are convened in England.

930 ASSEMBLY IN ICELAND
Vikings establish the Althing in Iceland. Today's Althing has the earliest foundation date of any modern legislature.

979 THE FIRST TYNWALD
Founding of the Tynwald, an assembly on the Isle of Man, now part of the UK. Today it is the oldest legislature with a continuous history.

1172 ELECTIONS IN VENICE
Committee of 40 appointed to elect the doge.

1188 THE SPANISH CORTES
The first representative assembly in Spain is the Cortes of Castile and León.

1215 MAGNA CARTA
King John of England signs a charter that limits royal powers and sets out rights for citizens.

1264 DE MONTFORT'S PARLIAMENT
Simon de Montfort summons England's first elected parliament—without royal assent.

1293 A SCOTTISH PARLIAMENT
Earliest surviving record of a parliament held in Scotland. By 1326 it included the Commons.

1307 FRENCH PARLIAMENT
The Parliament of Paris (representing all of France) develops from the royal court.

1404 PARLIAMENT IN WALES
Rebel leader Owain Glyndwr summons the first Welsh parliament in Machynlleth.

The Great Council Chamber of the republic of Venice, first used in 1419

Factories of the Industrial Age, which led to calls for workers to be given the vote

1493 POLAND'S PARLIAMENT
The Polish Sejm, an assembly that checked the monarchy, becomes more powerful.

1593 PARLIAMENT IN THE NETHERLANDS
The States-General meets in The Hague, with representatives from each Dutch province.

1642–1649 CROWN VS. PARLIAMENT
Civil War between the English parliament and royal supporters. Charles I is executed in 1649.

1649–1660 REPUBLICAN ENGLAND
England becomes a republic or Commonwealth.

1689 ENGLAND'S BILL OF RIGHTS
England becomes a constitutional monarchy.

1775 AMERICA BREAKS FREE
American Revolution breaks out. Independence is declared in 1776 and the US is founded as an independent republic in 1781.

1789 REVOLUTION IN FRANCE
The national assembly demands a constitution and starts the French Revolution.

1793–1794 REIGN OF TERROR
The French Revolution runs out of control, with mass executions. By 1804 France is an empire, ruled by the Emperor Napoléon I.

1807–1833 AN END TO SLAVERY
Slavery and the slave trade are abolished in the British empire. France follows in 1848.

1819 PETERLOO MASSACRE
Protesters demanding votes for all are killed at a rally in Manchester, England, the heart of the new Industrial Age.

1838 THE PEOPLE'S CHARTER
British protesters called Chartists set out their demands for radical reform.

1848 YEAR OF REVOLUTIONS
Struggles for democracy break out in Sicily, France, Vienna, Milan, Naples, Hungary, Germany, and Poland.

1861–1865 CIVIL WAR IN THE US
Slavery is a major issue in the American Civil War. Slavery was abolished in the US in 1865, but African Americans did not win the vote until 1870.

1867 CANADIAN PARLIAMENT
The parliament of Canada is established, with a Senate and a House of Commons.

1868 AMERICAN WOMEN CAMPAIGN
The American Equal Rights Association campaigns for women's suffrage.

1871 PARIS COMMUNE
Parisians set up a revolutionary direct democracy. It is suppressed after two months.

1893 NEW ZEALAND LEADS
Women vote for the first time in a general election, in New Zealand.

1901 FEDERAL AUSTRALIA
Australian colonies form one nation, with state and federal legislatures.

1903 SUFFRAGETTES
Emmeline Pankhurst founds the Women's Social and Political Union in the UK.

1906 WOMEN REPRESENTATIVES
Finland is the first country to elect women as members of parliament.

Medal of the Paris Commune, 1871

1914–1918 WORLD WAR I
A global conflict kills millions, devastates Europe, and creates new conflict.

1917 RUSSIAN REVOLUTIONS
Russia's February Revolution overthrows the monarchy and creates a parliament. An October Revolution hands power to the Bolsheviks.

1919 LEAGUE OF NATIONS
An international organization is founded to foster peace, diplomacy, security, and welfare.

1919–1945 FASCISM IN EUROPE
The rise of fascism in Italy and Nazism in Germany, both violently antidemocratic.

1920 US WOMEN WIN THE VOTE
The US extends the franchise to women.

1928–1953 STALINISM
Joseph Stalin gains control in the Soviet Union, beginning a reign of terror with secret police, show trials, and labor camps.

1929 UNIVERSAL FRANCHISE IN THE UK
The UK grants the vote to everyone over 21.

1936–1939 SPANISH CIVIL WAR
The Spanish republic is defeated by a fascist-conservative alliance led by Francisco Franco.

1939–1945 WORLD WAR II
War results in a defeat for fascism.

1945 UNITED NATIONS
The United Nations organization is founded to uphold international law, human rights, social progress, and economic development.

1945–1990 COLD WAR
A period of international tension and hostility between communist and capitalist nations.

1947 INDEPENDENCE FOR INDIA
India becomes the world's largest democracy.

1949 RED CHINA
A communist government rules the world's most populous nation.

1960 FIRST WOMAN LEADER
Sirimavo Bandaranaike of Ceylon (Sri Lanka) is the world's first woman prime minister.

1963 "I HAVE A DREAM"
US civil rights campaigner Dr. Martin Luther King Jr. outlines his vision of a nonracist future.

1968 THE PRAGUE SPRING
Czech leader Alexander Dubcek's liberal reforms are suppressed by a Soviet invasion.

1974–1975 RETURNS TO DEMOCRACY
Military rule ends in Greece, fascist rule ends in Portugal, and Spain's dictator Franco dies.

1979 EUROPE-WIDE ELECTIONS
The first direct elections to the European parliament are held in EU member states.

1985–1989 SOVIET REFORMS
Mikhail Gorbachev attempts reform in the Soviet Union, under the slogans of *glasnost* ("openness") and *perestroika* ("reconstruction").

1989 TIANANMEN SQUARE, BEIJING
Chinese troops kill demonstrators calling for democracy, rights, and economic safeguards.

1990–1991 END OF THE USSR
As the USSR and communist states in Eastern Europe collapse, new nations emerge, some of them democratic.

1994 SOUTH AFRICAN ELECTION
South Africa holds its first general election with votes for all citizens.

2000 US PRESIDENTIAL ELECTION
A contested result is decided by the Supreme Court in favor of Republican George W. Bush.

2005 IRAQI ELECTIONS
Following the US-led invasion that overthrew Saddam Hussein, elections are held, amid growing civil war.

2007 BURMA PROTESTS
Pro-democracy protesters clash with the military regime in Burma (Myanmar).

Buddhist monks march in Rangoon, Burma, in September 2007

Places to visit

US CAPITOL, WASHINGTON, DC
www.aoc.gov
The Capitol Guide Service conducts free guided tours, or US citizens may obtain passes to the galleries from their Representative or Senator.

ANCIENT AGORA MUSEUM, ATHENS
http://www.greece-museums.com/museum/33
The museum includes exhibits directly related to the theme of ancient Greek democracy.

EUROPEAN PARLIAMENT
www.europarl.europa.eu
Visit the European Parliament at its locations in Brussels, Strasbourg, and Luxembourg.

HOUSES OF PARLIAMENT, WESTMINSTER (LONDON), UK
www.parliament.uk
In summer there are paid tours for overseas visitors.

INTERNATIONAL SLAVERY MUSEUM, LIVERPOOL, UK
www.liverpoolmuseums.org.uk/ism
This museum tells the story of the slave trade and those who fought against slavery and for human rights and freedom.

MUSEUM OF LONDON, LONDON, UK
www.museumoflondon.org.uk
This museum houses material on the suffragettes, from the archive of the Women's Social and Political Union.

Bronze of a shackled slave, International Slavery Museum

Useful websites

• The Smithsonian Institution has a site dedicated to the history of voting methods:
http://americanhistory.si.edu/vote

• This site explains how US Congress works:
http://clerkkids.house.gov/congress/index.html

• This site has links to national parliaments around the world:
www.ipu.org/english/parlweb

• The Electoral Reform Society site explains how different voting systems work:
www.electoral-reform.org.uk

• Visit the BBC website to read about the first democracy—choose Athens and Democracy:
www.bbc.co.uk/history/ancient/greeks

A to Z of famous people

REFORMERS, REVOLUTIONARIES, philosophers, campaigners, lawmakers, statesmen, and writers... all have their place in the history of voting and democracy. So do the opponents of democracy—the dictators, tyrants, and absolute monarchs. However, democracy is not just about famous people. It is about all the ordinary people who struggled to win the vote and who used it to work toward social justice and liberty.

Statue of Abraham Lincoln, 16th US president

ANTHONY, SUSAN BROWNELL (1820–1906)
American Susan B. Anthony cofounded the National Women's Suffrage Association in 1869.

ARISTOTLE (384–322 BCE)
A student of Plato, this Greek philosopher excluded women, slaves, and manual laborers from citizenship and favored government by the middle class.

AUNG SAN SUU KYI (B. 1945)
Leader of the National League for Democracy in Burma (Myanmar), this politician won the 1990 election, but the country's military rulers refused to hand over power.

BABEUF, FRANÇOIS NOËL (1760–1797)
Known as "Gracchus" after his heroes, the Roman popular tribunes, Babeuf found fame in the French Revolution. Sometimes called an early communist, he believed in the sovereignty of the people and the freedom of the press.

BANDARANAIKE, SIRIMAVO (1916–2002)
"Mrs. B" was the first woman in the world to be elected as a prime minister, in 1960. She headed the government of Ceylon (now Sri Lanka) and was reelected for two further terms.

BOLÍVAR, SIMÓN (1783–1830)
Simón Bolívar was a South American freedom fighter, who won independence from Spain for the lands now known as Peru, Bolivia, Ecuador, Colombia, Venezuela, and Panama.

CROMWELL, OLIVER (1599–1658)
During the republican Commonwealth period, Cromwell governed Britain, crushed the radical democratic movement known as the Levellers, and launched a savage invasion of Ireland.

FAWCETT, MILLICENT GARRETT (1847–1929)
A leading educationalist and campaigner for women's votes, Fawcett rejected militant methods. She led the National Union of Women's Suffrage Societies from 1897 to 1919.

GARIBALDI, GIUSEPPE (1807–1882)
A freedom fighter in South America and Europe, Garibaldi helped to bring about a united Italy. He campaigned for universal suffrage (votes for all).

GORBACHEV, MIKHAIL (B. 1931)
The last leader of the USSR (1985–1991), Gorbachev brought in democratic reforms, known as *glasnost* ("openness") and *perestroika* ("reconstruction").

GRACCHUS, TIBERIUS (163–132 BCE) AND GAIUS (154–121 BCE)
These two brothers were tribunes (officials) who represented the ordinary people of Rome. They tried to bring in democratic reforms and to limit the power of the big landowners in order to protect small farmers. They were both killed by political opponents.

HITLER, ADOLF (1889–1945)
Adolf Hitler led the German Nazi Party, which gained electoral success through intimidation and propaganda. Defeated in World War II, he committed suicide in 1945.

JEFFERSON, THOMAS (1743–1826)
A founder of the US, Jefferson drafted the Declaration of Independence and served as third president of the US (1801–1809).

KING, MARTIN LUTHER JR. (1929–1968)
This African American pastor championed civil rights in the US in the 1950s and '60s. He helped to secure the passing of the Voting Rights Act in 1965. He was assassinated in 1968.

KLEISTHENES OF ATHENS (C. 560–C. 500 BCE)
The father of democracy in ancient Athens, Kleisthenes enlarged the people's council and extended the rights of the citizens' assembly.

LENIN, VLADIMIR ILYICH (1870–1924)
A Russian revolutionary inspired by the writings of Marx and Engels, Lenin led his Bolsheviks to power in the revolution of October 1917. He was one of the founders of the Soviet Union.

LINCOLN, ABRAHAM (1809–1865)
The 16th president of the US, Lincoln led the victorious Union government during the Civil War (1861–1865), which resulted in an end to slavery. He was assassinated in 1865.

LOCKE, JOHN (1632–1704)
This English philosopher supported natural rights, individual liberty, religious toleration, and government by the consent of the people.

MADISON, JAMES (1751–1836)
Principal author of the US Constitution and Bill of Rights, Madison went on to serve as fourth US president.

MANDELA, NELSON (B. 1918)
This anti-apartheid campaigner joined the African National Congress in 1944. Imprisoned from 1964 to 1990, he became South Africa's first black president (1994–1999).

MAO ZEDONG (1893–1976)
Mao was a founder of the Chinese Communist Party, which came to power in 1949. He introduced radical land reform and industrial development that led to mass starvation and economic disasters.

Writing desk of US suffragist Susan B. Anthony

Figurine of Chinese leader Mao Zedong

MARX, KARL (1818–1883)
With Friedrich Engels, this German philosopher and economist wrote the *Communist Manifesto* (1848). Marx believed that only a revolution led by the workers could end capitalist exploitation and usher in a communist society.

MILL, JOHN STUART (1806–1873)
A liberal English social reformer, Mill campaigned for women's right to vote, the extension of the franchise, proportional representation, and workers' rights.

MONTFORT, SIMON DE (1208–1265)
This powerful English baron rebelled against Henry III in 1263–1264. He established himself and two others as rulers of the country, but set up a directly elected parliament as well.

MUSSOLINI, BENITO (1883–1945)
A founder of Italian fascism, Mussolini was dictator of Italy by 1929. He was captured and shot by opponents during World War II.

PAINE, THOMAS (1737–1809)
This English writer supported the American struggle for independence. He published *The Rights of Man* (1791–1792), which called for the overthrow of the monarchy.

Eva Perón, who helped to secure the franchise for Argentinian women in 1952

PANKHURST, EMMELINE (1857–1928)
An English campaigner for women's votes, Pankhurst founded the Women's Franchise League in 1889 and the militant Women's Social and Political Union (WSPU) in 1903.

PERIKLES (C. 495–429 BCE)
Perikles was the greatest statesman of ancient Athens and a brilliant orator. He was a radical democrat, repeatedly voted in as military leader by the citizens' assembly. He ensured that poorer people could hold public office by offering them payment for their work.

PERÓN, EVA (1919–1952)
Originally an actress, "Evita" became the second wife of Argentinian president Juan Perón, a ruthless populist who admired Mussolini. She worked to address social injustice and founded the Female Peronist Party. Just before her death, she ran for vice-president with huge support.

PLATO (C. 427–347 BCE)
This Greek philosopher opposed the democracy of his day. He argued that only a philosophically-trained guardian class was competent to rule.

RAWLS, JOHN (1921–2002)
This US philosopher defended liberal freedoms and social justice as the basis of agreement between people in societies divided by religion and culture.

Death of Wat Tyler during the Peasants' Revolt, 1381

ROUSSEAU, JEAN-JACQUES (1712–1778)
This Swiss-born philosopher claimed that people would only be free when they were governed by the general will. He proposed direct democracy rather than representative assemblies and inspired many revolutionaries.

SOKRATES (C. 470–399 BCE)
A Greek philosopher who despised democracy and believed that only the philosophical search for truth could produce political wisdom. The people's assembly sentenced him to death for dangerous teaching.

SOLON (C. 638–559 BCE)
This Greek lawmaker made the lower classes full voting citizens of Athens and set up the 400-member people's council. The purpose of his reforms was *eunomia* ("good order").

STALIN, JOSEPH (1879–1953)
Following the death of Lenin, Stalin rose to power in the Soviet Union. He forced through reforms that resulted in countless deaths, but led his country to victory in World War II.

STANTON, ELIZABETH CADY (1815–1902)
An American campaigner for the abolition of slavery and for women's voting rights, Stanton organized the first women's rights convention, in 1848. She became president of the National American Woman Suffrage Association in 1890.

TOCQUEVILLE, ALEXIS DE (1805–1859)
French historian, lawyer, and politician Tocqueville wrote *Democracy in America* (1835) and *The Old Regime and the Revolution* (1856), but during the unrest of 1848 he spoke against the political freedoms he had once supported.

TRUTH, SOJOURNER (C. 1797–1883)
Born an African American slave, Truth was a leading campaigner for the abolition of slavery, for women's suffrage, and prison reform.

TYLER, WAT (D. 1381)
Leader of the Peasants' Revolt (1381), a 20,000-strong rebellion demanding fair taxation, Tyler was killed on orders of London's mayor.

VOLTAIRE (1694–1778)
Born François-Marie Arouet, this French writer was a leading thinker of the Enlightenment, who supported social reform and civil liberties.

WEBB, BEATRICE (1858–1943)
With her husband Sidney Webb, this British economist and social reformer helped to establish the London School of Economics and founded the Fabian Society. The Fabians believed in reform rather than revolution, and influenced the policies of the Labour Party.

WILBERFORCE, WILLIAM (1759–1833)
This English member of parliament campaigned against slavery in the British empire, as well as on moral and Christian issues, and on animal welfare. He was opposed to trade unionism.

WILKES, JOHN (1725–1797)
This English member of parliament called for reform of the legislature, published reports of parliamentary proceedings, and voters' rights in selection of representatives.

WOLLSTONECRAFT, MARY (1759–1797)
This Anglo-Irish reformer wrote *Vindication of the Rights of Man* (1790) and *Vindication of the Rights of Woman* (1792). She called for a society based on reason, education for women, and equality between the sexes, a proposal that later inspired the women's suffrage movement.

Bust of Voltaire, whose writings helped to inspire the French Revolution

Glossary

ABSOLUTE POWER Unchecked power, as held by a dictator, tyrant, or some monarchs.

AFFILIATION Joining or formally supporting a political party, alliance, or organization.

ANARCHIST Someone opposed to state power and centralized government, preferring society to be organized by voluntary democratic organizations such as community councils or trade unions.

ARMS RACE A competition between countries to gain military superiority through armaments, as happened during the Cold War.

ASSEMBLY (1) Any gathering of people. (2) A legislature such as a parliament.

ASYLUM (1) Any refuge from violence or persecution. (2) The protection offered by one country to a refugee from another.

BOYCOTT To refuse to buy certain goods or use certain services as a form of protest.

BY-ELECTION A subsidiary election—for example, one held between general elections to fill a seat that has become vacant.

CABINET A council of ministers or others that advises a head of government.

CAPITAL (1) The chief city of a nation, state, or region. (2) The wealth of a company or an individual, owned or used in business.

CAPITALISM An economic system in which the means of production, distribution, and exchange are mostly privately owned, and in which goods and services are exchanged by means of a free market.

CAPITOL (1) A famous building in ancient Rome. (2) The building of the legislature in the US and some other countries.

Figurine of a Russian woman stitching a communist banner

CAUCUS A committee within a political party based on region, ethnicity, or common interests.

CENSORSHIP The suppression of free expression—for example, in the media. It may be on the grounds of politics, business interests, public security, or morality.

CENTER GROUND A term that describes policies said to be moderate, not extreme.

CITIZENSHIP (1) The activities associated with the rights and duties of being a good citizen. (2) Official recognition as being a member of a particular territory or nation.

CITY-STATE A small, self-governing city, as in ancient Greece or Renaissance Italy.

CIVIL DISOBEDIENCE A refusal, as a matter of principle, to obey a law or pay a tax.

CIVIL RIGHTS The rights of the individual as a citizen, such as voting or equal opportunities.

CIVIL SOCIETY Those people who form nongovernmental organizations, voluntary associations, charities, and campaigning groups.

CIVIL WAR War between two factions within a single country.

COALITION A temporary alliance or union. In a coalition government, different political parties agree to work and govern together.

COLONY A territory settled by or governed by another nation.

COMMUNE (1) A small administrative division of a country. (2) A social or political group founded on shared wealth, cooperation, or common aims. (3) The revolutionary government formed in Paris in 1871.

COMMUNISM A political ideology that aims to create a classless society, with communal or state ownership of the means of production.

CONSERVATIVE (1) Favoring traditional institutions and wary of change. (2) Describing a political party that is opposed to socialism.

CONSTITUENCY (1) The group of people represented by the elected member of a legislature. (2) The area in which they live.

CONSTITUTION The laws that set out the principles by which a nation is governed.

CORRUPTION Abuses of a political system, such as dishonesty or bribery.

COUP D'ÉTAT A sudden political action against a state, especially the illegal or violent seizure of power.

DEBATE (1) Any public discussion. (2) A formal policy discussion in a meeting or assembly that concludes with a vote.

DELEGATE Somebody sent to an assembly to represent the views of another group of people.

Badge of the Nazi Party, which was inspired by fascism

DEMOCRACY Rule by the people (direct democracy), or by elected representatives of the people (representative or indirect democracy).

DEVOLUTION The passing of powers from central government to other tiers (or layers) of government, such as regional assemblies.

DICTATOR A ruler who has absolute power.

DISSENT Disagreement, opposition.

ELECTORAL Relating to an election.

ELECTRONIC VOTING Counting votes by means of electronic systems such as optical scanning, punch cards, direct electronic recording, or votes via the Internet or telephone.

EXECUTIVE The part of a government that makes political decisions and acts on them.

EXILE Being sent away from one's country.

FASCISM An authoritarian political system based on dictatorship, centralized power, militarism, and extreme nationalism.

FEDERAL (1) Based on a political union of states or territories, in which there is a centralized legislature in addition to regional legislatures. (2) Representing the centralized government in such a system.

FIRST-PAST-THE-POST An electoral system in which the candidate or party gaining the most votes wins outright.

Horse race, won by the first horse to pass the finishing post

FRANCHISE The right to vote.

GENERAL ELECTION A major election for a national or federal legislature, as opposed to a presidential election or a local election.

GOVERNMENT (1) Political rule and administration, directing the affairs of state. (2) A body that carries out these functions.

HEAD OF STATE The chief representative of a nation, such as a monarch or president. He or she may have only symbolic powers, limited by the constitution, or full executive powers.

HUMAN RIGHTS The basic rights to which all people are entitled, including life, liberty, security, and the resources to lead a decent life.

IDEOLOGY A set of theories and practical ideas intended to achieve a political end—for example, conservatism or socialism.

INVEST To put money into a program or a project in the hope of making a profit or earning interest, or of helping other people.

JUDICIARY The branch of the state (generally separate from government) responsible for justice and implementing the law.

LEFT-WING In favor of political change and greater equality in society.

LEGISLATION Law-making or laws.

LEGISLATURE Any assembly that makes or revises laws, such as a parliament.

LIBERAL (1) Progressive or reforming. (2) With few restrictions on the freedom of the individual.

LOBBY To try to persuade a body such as a government to follow a particular policy.

MAJORITY The larger part, having the greater number of votes or parliamentary seats.

MARXISM A system of thought based on the writings of Karl Marx, which claim that a ruling class exploits the mass of workers, that class struggle has always been an agent of change, and that capitalism cannot survive.

MEDIA The various means of public communications, including broadcasting, the press, telecommunications, and the Internet.

MILITANT Politically active and combative.

MILITARIST Seeking military solutions.

MINORITY The smaller part, having fewer votes or parliamentary seats.

MONARCHY Hereditary rule by a single person, such as a king. An absolute monarch has unchecked powers. A constitutional monarch has limited powers.

Gavel, a symbol of the judiciary

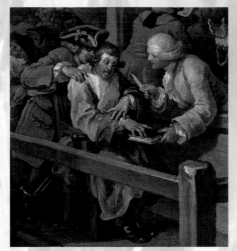

Detail from a Hogarth painting that uses satire to show the failings of the polling system

NATIONALIST (1) Someone seeking independence as a nation for a particular territory, such as a colony or a region. (2) Someone who emphasizes the superiority of their own nation above others.

ONE-PARTY STATE A nation in which one political party dominates government.

OPPOSITION (1) Taking a position against a government, organization, or policy. (2) The party or parties in a legislature that are not in government.

PARLIAMENT A legislative assembly, generally made up of one or two houses or chambers.

PHILOSOPHER Someone who makes a systematic study of the truths that underlie human existence and knowledge.

PLURALIST Having many political parties.

POLITICAL PARTY An organization of people with a common agenda or ideology, who campaign politically or seek election to legislatures.

POLITICS (1) Tactics for bringing about social or economic change. (2) Matters relating to government or international relations.

POLL (1) Voting at an election. (2) The number of votes made at an election. (3) An "opinion poll," in which voters are asked their opinions.

POLLING STATION The building in which people vote during an election.

PRESIDENT (1) A constitutional head of state with limited powers (as in Germany or Ireland). (2) A head of state with extensive executive powers (as in the US).

PRIME MINISTER The head of government in a parliamentary democracy (answering to the head of state).

PROPAGANDA Persuasive, often misleading information.

PROPORTIONAL REPRESENTATION Any voting system that attempts to ensure that parties win seats in proportion to their shares of the national vote.

RACIST Believing that humanity is divided into races and that some are superior to others.

RADICAL Fundamental, going to the root of a problem, and neither moderate nor superficial.

REFERENDUM A form of direct democracy in which a vote is taken on a particular issue.

REPRESENTATIVE Someone who is voted in to represent the public in a legislature—for example, a member of parliament.

REPUBLIC A nation that is governed in the name of the people, not a hereditary monarch.

REVOLUTION (1) The overthrow of a political system or government, often by force. (2) A period of great social, economic, or cultural change.

RIGHT-WING In favor of tradition, social order, and established authority.

SATIRE The use of humor or ridicule to expose foolishness or corruption.

SEGREGATION Keeping certain social groups apart from each other—for example, on account of their race or religion.

SENATE (1) A form of legislative assembly, as in ancient Rome. (2) The upper house of a legislative assembly, as in the US or Ireland.

SLAVE Someone owned as property and forced to work without pay.

CCTV, used for surveillance

SOCIALISM A political system that favors state ownership, not capitalism.

SUFFRAGE The right to vote. Universal suffrage means votes for all.

SUFFRAGETTE A radical campaigner for women's votes.

SUFFRAGIST A moderate campaigner for women's votes.

SUPPRESS To put down a rebellion, end a practice, or block information.

SURVEILLANCE Keeping watch over people—for example, by using bugs or CCTV.

TOTALITARIAN Allowing no opposition and bringing all aspects of social life under state control.

TRADE UNION An association of working people that aims to protect or improve working conditions and wages.

TYRANNY (1) In ancient Greece, rule by any nonhereditary leader with absolute powers. (2) Rule characterized by oppression.

WARD The division of a city or town that forms a constituency in municipal elections.

Index

Acknowledgments

Dorling Kindersley would like to thank
Peter Winfield for illustrations 42bl, 64–65; Stewart J. Wild for proofreading; Hilary Bird for the index; David Ekholm-JAlbum, Claire Ellerton, Sunita Gahir, Susan St. Louis, Lisa Stock, & Bulent Yusuf for the clip art; Rob Houston & Susan St. Louis for the wall chart; Christine Heilman & Margaret Parrish for Americanization.

The publisher would like to thank the following for their kind permission to reproduce their photographs:
(a-above b-below/bottom c-center l-left r-right t-top)
akg-images: 22–23tc, 25cra, 28–29c, 30tr, 30–31c; Accademia di Brera 22–23b; John Hios 10br, 11bl; Pirozzi 11br; **Alamy Images:** Alaska Stock LLC 59cc; Don Hammond/Design Pics Inc. 51bl; Mary Evans Picture Library 13tl, 22bl; Ray Roberts 11tl; The Print Collector 13tl; vario images GmbH & Co.KG 44cb; Zak Waters 47tr; Peter M. Wilson 10t; David Wootton 57bl; **Amnesty International UK:** 50cl; **The Art Archive:** Bodleian Library Oxford 24–25b; Culver Pictures 16–17c; Museo Bolivar Caracas / Gianni Dagli Orti 25tl; Museum of the City of New York / 46l22.5.12 27bl; National Archives Washington DC 16l; Eileen Tweedy 22cl; **The Bridgeman Art Library:** 71t; British Museum 15tc;

Chateau de Versailles, France, Giraudon 19bc; Collection of the New-York Historical Society, USA 21c; Courtesy of the Trustees of Sir John Soane's Museum, London 15b; Musee de la Ville de Paris, Musee Carnavalet, Paris, France, Giraudon 19br; Private Collection 14br, 21tl, 31tl; Private Collection, Archives Charmet 16tl, 25tr; **The Trustees of the British Museum:** 1285tr; **Christie's Images Ltd.:** 23cr; **Corbis:** Pallava Bagla 6b; Bettmann 14t, 17c, 21br, 25c, 28bc, 28bl, 28cr, 31tc, 32tr, 33tl, 34tl, 68l; Jack Dabaghian / Reuters 36l; Larry Downing / Reuters 46tl; Najlah Feanny 9c; Rahmat Gul / epa 35tl; Hulton-Deutsch Collection 30br; Nilo Jimenez / epa 35tr; Kopczynski / Reuters 41tr; Jason Lee / Reuters 43r; Matthew McKee 33tr; Michael Nicholson 26c; Kerim Okten / epa 53cr; Caroline Penn 63tl; Reuters 29br, 46b; Jorge Silva/Reuters 64tr; Luc Skeudener / epa 8c; David Smith 48bl; Swim Ink 30tl; Tetra Images 17tl; Goran Tomasevic / Reuters 34tr; Peter Turnley 33br, 44br; Arnd Wiegmann / Reuters 42l; Alexandra Winkler / Reuters 46tr; Valdrin Xhemaj / epa 40–41c; **DK Images:** Academy of Motion Picture Arts and Sciences 4tl, 61c; Courtesy of Amnesty International 55bl; The British Museum 69tr; Sean Hunter 15tr; Courtesy of Old North Church, Boston 4cl, 16br; Wilberforce House/Hull Museums 20–

21c; **Getty Images:** 21tr; Adrian Bradshaw 53c; The Bridgeman Art Library 18bl, 18br, 19bl, 26l; William Thomas Cain 60br; Niall Carson/AFP 8b; Emmanuel Dunand / AFP 35br; Johannes Eisele / AFP 48–49c; Sezayi Erken / AFP 50–51c; Novaya Gazeta 35bl; Dirck Halstead 45c; Alexander Joe / AFP 34bc; Joe Klamar / AFP 8–9b; Carsten Koall 52l; Teh Eng Koon 61cl; Steve McAlister 8tl; David McNew 45bl; Scott Olson 51tr; Jan Pitman 31tr; Roger L. Wollenberg-Pool 37bl; Raveendran/AFP 6c; Andreas Rentz 45t; Seyllou / AFP 47cr; Prakash Singh/AFP 6–7c; Chip Somodevilla 42t; Rizwan Tabassum / AFP 52c; Time & Life Pictures 32b; Travelpix Ltd 39bl; Ian Waldie 38–39c; **Greenpeace:** 50cla; **Image courtesy of International Slavery Museum:** 67r; **iStockphoto.com:** 52tr; **Mary Evans Picture Library:** 44tr; The Women's Library 26br, 27c; **NASA:** 63br; **North Wind Picture Archives:** 49tc; Nancy Carter 17tr; **PA Photos:** Remy De La Mauviniere/AP 52–53c; Ted S. Warren/AP 47br; Associated Press 67b; Frank Augstein/AP 60bl; Rebecca Blackwell/AP 56–57c; Jean Blondin 43b; Khampha Bouaphanh/AP 57br; Charlie Neibergall/AP 40bl; Elizabeth Dalziel/AP 54bl; Richard Drew/AP 58tr; Fabrizo Giovannozzi/AP 55tl; Hamid Jalaludin/AP 54cr; Kamran Jebreili/AP 60cl; David Jones 44bl; Jerry Lampen/AP 36bc; Brennan Linsley/AP 56bl; Kevin Martin/AP 57cr; Jacky Naegelen/AP 43tl; Anupam Nath/AP 47bl; Gurinder Osan/AP 7tc; Lefteris Pitarakis/AP 63cr; Karel Prinsloo/AP 58br; Rick Rycroft/AP 56br; Paul Sakuma/AP 61br; Joerg Sarbach/AP 59tr; Reed Saxon/AP 54br; Edmond

Terakopian 53t; Ed Wray/AP 58cl; **PhotoNewZealand:** 26tc; **Réunion des Musées Nationaux Agence Photographique:** Bulloz 18–19tc, 21bl; **Reuters:** 37tr; Marcel Bieri 45br; B Mathur 7tr; Tim Shaffer 53br; Str Old 49br; Stringer Spain 57br; Stringer Taiwan 39c; **Rex Features:** Paul Cooper 59tl; Philip Dunn 63l; David Hartley 61bl; Sipa Press 54tr, 64–65c; Venturelli 61tr; Geoff Wilkinson 41br; **The Ronald Grant Archive:** 9tr; **Richard Solomon:** CF Payne 40–41bc; **TopFoto.co.uk:** 27br, 29cr; The British Library/HIP 12–13b; ImageWorks 50tr; Museum of London/HIP 14l; **UN/DPI Photo:** Mark Garten 63t.
Wall chart: Alamy Images: Mary Evans Picture Library bl (suffragette); Corbis: Reuters ca; Tetra Images cl (Liberty Bell); DK Images: Stephen Oliver clb (Little Red Book), crb (newspapers); Rough Guides ftl; By kind permission of the Trustees of the Wallace Collection cla (Cromwell); Getty Images: Francis Miller/Time Life Pictures fbl; Reuters: Jean Blondin JD crb (Moroccan Parliament).
Jacket: Front: Alamy Images: Graham Hughes (ftr); Phil Wahlbrink (tr); Pictorial Press (tl). Corbis: Araldo de Luca (tcr); David J. & Janice L. Frent Collection (tca); Shepard Sherbell (b). Reuters: (tl). **Back:** Alamy Images: Mary Evans Picture Library (cr, l); Jeremy Hoare (cla). Corbis: Bettmann (tr); William Whitehurst (cra); Reuters (tc); David Turnley (br); William Whitehurst (cra). PunchStock: Cut and Deal Ltd (c).

All other images © Dorling Kindersley
For further information see: www.dkimages.com